First World War
and Army of Occupation
War Diary
France, Belgium and Germany

16 DIVISION
49 Infantry Brigade
Royal Inniskilling Fusiliers
7/8th Battalion
1 September 1917 - 31 May 1918

WO95/1977/4

The Naval & Military Press Ltd
www.nmarchive.com
Published in association with The National Archives

Published by

The Naval & Military Press Ltd

Unit 10 Ridgewood Industrial Park,

Uckfield, East Sussex,

TN22 5QE England

Tel: +44 (0) 1825 749494

www.naval-military-press.com

www.nmarchive.com

This diary has been reprinted in facsimile from the original. Any imperfections are inevitably reproduced and the quality may fall short of modern type and cartographic standards.

© Crown Copyright
Images reproduced by permission of The National Archives, London, England, 2015.

Contents

Document type	Place/Title	Date From	Date To
Heading	1977/4 7/8 Battalion Royal Iniskilling Fusiliers Sept 1917-May 1918		
Heading	16 Division 49 Inf Bde 7/8 Bn Royal Inniskilling Fusiliers 1917 Sep-1918 May To 30 Div 89 Bde		
Heading	War Diary. For Month Of September, 1917. Volume 1 Unit 7/8th Btn R. Inniskilling Fuslrs.		
War Diary	Ervillers No. 5 Camp	01/09/1917	16/09/1917
War Diary	Ervillers	16/09/1917	16/09/1917
War Diary	Rt. Support	28/09/1917	28/09/1917
Heading	War Diary For Month Of October, 1917. Unit 7/8 Btn R. Inniskilling Fus Volume Number 2		
War Diary	Rt. Support	01/10/1917	01/10/1917
War Diary	Front Line	04/10/1917	10/10/1917
War Diary	Enniskillen Camp	11/10/1917	22/10/1917
War Diary	Right Support	22/10/1917	28/10/1917
War Diary	Front Line	28/10/1917	29/10/1917
War Diary		01/10/1917	29/10/1917
Operation(al) Order(s)	49th Infantry Brigade Order No. 173 Appendix "A"	27/10/1917	27/10/1917
Map	Artillery & T.M. Barrage Map 49th Inf Bde Raid		
Miscellaneous	All recipients of 49th Inf. Bde. Order No. 173 49th Inf. Bde. No. B.C. 173/2-30-10-17 Appendix "B"	30/10/1917	30/10/1917
Heading	War Diary For Month Of November, 1917 Volume:- 3 Unit:- 7th/8th R. Inniskilling Fus.		
War Diary	Enniskillen Camp	01/11/1917	14/11/1917
War Diary	Front Line	15/11/1917	18/11/1917
War Diary	Support	19/11/1917	21/11/1917
War Diary	Front Line	21/11/1917	25/11/1917
War Diary	Front Line	22/11/1917	22/11/1917
War Diary	Enniskillen Camp	25/11/1917	30/11/1917
War Diary		17/11/1917	24/11/1917
War Diary		12/11/1917	27/11/1917
Heading	War Diary For Month Of December, 1917. Volume:- 4 Unit:- 7/8th Inniskilling Fusiliers.		
War Diary	Croisilles Sector Support	01/12/1917	02/12/1917
War Diary	Ervillers	02/12/1917	03/12/1917
War Diary	Barastre	03/12/1917	05/12/1917
War Diary	Buire	05/12/1917	06/12/1917
War Diary	Ste Emelie	06/12/1917	12/12/1917
War Diary	Front Line	12/12/1917	17/12/1917
War Diary	Tincourt	17/12/1917	23/12/1917
War Diary	Lempire Defences	23/12/1917	29/12/1917
War Diary	Front Line	29/12/1917	04/01/1918
War Diary	Villers-Faucon	04/01/1918	10/01/1918
War Diary	St Emelie	10/01/1918	16/01/1918
War Diary	Front Line	16/01/1918	22/01/1918
War Diary	Support	22/01/1918	28/01/1918
War Diary	Front Line	28/01/1918	31/01/1918
War Diary		09/01/1918	13/01/1918
War Diary		05/01/1918	28/01/1918
War Diary		10/01/1918	10/01/1918

Miscellaneous	49th Inf. Bde. No. B.M.C. 13/233-17.1.18	17/01/1918	17/01/1918
Miscellaneous	49th Inf. Brigade.	17/01/1918	17/01/1918
Miscellaneous	49th Inf. Bde. No. B.M.C. 13/233/1 17.1.18	17/01/1918	17/01/1918
Miscellaneous	Headquarters, 49th Infantry Brigade.	17/01/1918	17/01/1918
Miscellaneous	Headquarters, 49th Inf. Brigade.	17/01/1918	17/01/1918
Map	Dispositions 16/1/18 7/8th R Innis Fus		
Heading	War Diary. For Month Of February. 1918. Volume:- 6 Unit:- 7/8th Ro Inniskilling Fusrs.		
War Diary	Front Line	01/02/1918	03/02/1918
War Diary	Divisional Reserve	03/02/1918	07/02/1918
War Diary	Bgde Reserve	14/02/1918	18/02/1918
War Diary		08/02/1918	17/02/1918
War Diary		14/02/1918	29/02/1918
War Diary	Front Line	18/02/1918	28/02/1918
War Diary	Support	28/02/1918	28/02/1918
Heading	49th Brigade. 16th Division. 7/8th Battalion Royal Inniskilling Fusiliers March 1918		
War Diary	St Emilie	01/03/1918	02/03/1918
War Diary	Ronnsoy	08/03/1918	21/03/1918
War Diary			
Miscellaneous	Raid on 7th-/8th Inniskillings on night 4th-/5th March.	04/03/1918	04/03/1918
Miscellaneous			
Miscellaneous	H.Q. 49th Inf. Bde. (Brigade Major)	07/03/1918	07/03/1918
Miscellaneous	H.Q. 49th Inf Bde. (Brigade Major)	05/03/1918	05/03/1918
War Diary	E.U.	04/04/1918	30/04/1918
War Diary	Steenbecque	15/05/1918	31/05/1918
Heading	Cover for Documents. Nature of Enclosures. 49th Infantry Brigade Administrative Instructions.		
Miscellaneous	49th Infantry Brigade Special Administrative Instructions.		
Miscellaneous	49th Infantry Brigade Special Administrative Instructions. No. 1	03/07/1917	03/07/1917
Operation(al) Order(s)	8th. R. Inniskilling Fusiliers Operation Order No. 111-7/7/17	07/07/1917	07/07/1917
Operation(al) Order(s)	8th. R. Inniskilling Fusiliers Operation Order No. 112-8/7/17	08/07/1917	08/07/1917
Miscellaneous	49th Infantry Brigade. Special Administrative Instruction No. 4. Burial Orders.	15/07/1917	15/07/1917
Miscellaneous	Burial Return 16th. Division. (Pro-Forma).		
Miscellaneous	49th Infantry Brigade. Special Administrative Instructions No. 5. Salvage.	16/07/1917	16/07/1917
Miscellaneous	49th Infantry Brigade. Special Administrative Instructions No. 7. Medical Arrangements.	16/07/1917	16/07/1917
Miscellaneous	49th Infantry Brigade. Special Administrative Instructions No. 3. Accommodation.	16/07/1917	16/07/1917
Operation(al) Order(s)	8th. Royal Inniskilling Fusiliers Operation Order No. 113.- 24/7/17	24/07/1917	24/07/1917
Operation(al) Order(s)	8th. Royal Inniskilling Fusiliers Operation Order No. 114.- 27-7-17	27/07/1917	27/07/1917
Miscellaneous	8th R. Innis. Fus. O.O. 114/1-29/7/17	29/07/1917	29/07/1917
Miscellaneous	8th R. Innis. Fus. S/539-30-7-17 Administrative Instructions.	30/07/1917	30/07/1917
Map	Boundary XIX Corps Area.		
Miscellaneous	H.Q. 49th. I.B.	23/07/1917	23/07/1917

Miscellaneous	49th Infantry Brigade. Special Administrative Instruction No. 10. Collection And Escort Of Prisoners Of War.	21/07/1917	21/07/1917
Miscellaneous	49th Infantry Brigade. Special Administrative Instruction No. 11. Ordnance Service.	21/07/1917	21/07/1917
Miscellaneous	49th Infantry Brigade. Special Administrative Instruction No. 12. March Discipline.	21/07/1917	21/07/1917
Miscellaneous	49th Infantry Brigade. Special Administrative Instruction No. 13. Veterinary Arrangements.	21/07/1917	21/07/1917
Miscellaneous	49th Infantry Brigade. Special Administrative Instructions. Amendments.	21/07/1917	21/07/1917
Miscellaneous	49th Infantry Brigade. Special Administrative Instruction No. 9. Reinforcement Depot.	17/07/1917	17/07/1917
Miscellaneous	A Form Messages And Signals		
Miscellaneous			
Miscellaneous	49th. I.B. No. S.C.C. 9/284 2nd. R. Irish. Regt.	17/07/1917	17/07/1917
Miscellaneous	Messages And Signals		
Miscellaneous	49th Infantry Brigade. Special Administrative Instruction No. 2. Organization Of Pack Transport.	24/07/1917	24/07/1917
Miscellaneous	Billeting List. To accompany 49th Inf. Bde. Administrative Instruction No. 13	25/07/1917	25/07/1917
Miscellaneous	49th Infantry Brigade Special Administrative Instructions. No. 8. Police Arrangements For Straggler Posts.	23/07/1917	23/07/1917
Miscellaneous	49th Infantry Brigade Appendix "A" To Special Administrative Instruction No. 3	23/07/1917	23/07/1917
Miscellaneous	49th Infantry Brigade. Special Administrative Instructions. Amendments.	28/07/1917	28/07/1917
Miscellaneous	49th Infantry Brigade. Special Administrative Instructions No. 13	22/07/1917	22/07/1917
Miscellaneous	n Cancel 49th Infantry Brigade Special Administrative Instruction No. 6, 6A, and 6B, for which the attached S.A.I. No. 6 is substituted.	25/07/1917	25/07/1917
Miscellaneous	49th Infantry Brigade. Special Administrative Instruction. No. 6. Water Supply	25/07/1917	25/07/1917
Miscellaneous	49th Infantry Brigade. Appendix "A" To Special Administrative Instruction. No. 10. Orders For Guards Over Prisoners Of War.	26/07/1917	26/07/1917
Miscellaneous	49th Infantry Brigade. Appendix "B" To Special Administrative Instruction. No. 10. Orders For Officers Or N.C. OS In Command Of Escorts To Prisoners Of War.	25/07/1917	25/07/1917
Miscellaneous	49th Infantry Brigade. Special Administrative Instruction No. 8. (Part 2).	26/07/1917	26/07/1917
Diagram etc	Brandhoek Area		
Miscellaneous	49th Infantry Brigade. Special Administrative Instructions. Amendments.	26/07/1917	26/07/1917
Miscellaneous	49th Infantry Brigade. Special Administrative Instructions. Amendment.	29/07/1917	29/07/1917
Miscellaneous	49th Infantry Brigade. Special Administrative Instruction. Amendment.	07/08/1917	07/08/1917
Miscellaneous	49th Infantry Brigade. Special Administrative Instruction. No. 14. Reporting Of Casualties.	29/07/1917	29/07/1917
Miscellaneous	8th. R. Innis. Fus. S/539-30-7-17 Administrative Instructions	30/07/1917	30/07/1917

Miscellaneous	49th Infantry Brigade. Appendix "A" to Special Administrative Instructions. No. 4	31/07/1917	31/07/1917
Miscellaneous	49th Infantry Brigade. Appendix "A" to Special Administrative Instructions. No. 7	31/07/1917	31/07/1917
Miscellaneous	49th Inf. Bde. No. S.S. 47-19-7-17	19/07/1917	19/07/1917
Miscellaneous	49th Inf. Bde. No. S.S. 47/2-21-7-17	21/07/1917	21/07/1917
Miscellaneous	O.C. "A" Coy	20/07/1917	20/07/1917
Miscellaneous	B Coy	20/07/1917	20/07/1917
Heading	To Adjutant		
Miscellaneous	O.C. "D" Coy.	20/07/1917	20/07/1917
Miscellaneous	Lieut. W.F. E 1/1S. M.C.	23/07/1917	23/07/1917
Miscellaneous	2/Lt. K.H. Borchers.	23/07/1917	23/07/1917
Miscellaneous	To Adjutant B.A.B. Code. Copy no. 11440 renewed.	23/07/1917	23/07/1917
Miscellaneous	49th Inf. Bde. No. S.O. 100-21-7-17	21/07/1917	21/07/1917
Miscellaneous	49th Infantry Brigade Instructions For The Offensive.	22/06/1917	22/06/1917
Miscellaneous	49th Infantry Brigade Instructions For The Offensive. Instructions No. 2	23/06/1917	23/06/1917
Miscellaneous	49th I.B. No. S.C.C. 2/128 2/R. Irish Regt.	08/08/1917	08/08/1917
Miscellaneous	49th Infantry Brigade Instructions For The Offensive. Instructions No. 3	23/07/1917	23/07/1917
Miscellaneous	49th Infantry Brigade Instructions For The Offensive. Instructions No. 4	24/07/1917	24/07/1917
Miscellaneous	49th Inf. Bde. No. S.O. 100/1-25-7-17	25/07/1917	25/07/1917
Miscellaneous	Following Dumps Will Be Formed By 15th. Division.		
Miscellaneous	49th Inf. Bde. No. S.O. 100/2-26-7-17	26/07/1917	26/07/1917
Miscellaneous	49th Infantry Brigade. Instructions For The Offensive. Instruction No. 5	25/07/1917	25/07/1917
Miscellaneous	49th Inf. Bde. No. S.O. 100/3-27-7-17	27/07/1917	27/07/1917
Miscellaneous	49th Infantry Brigade Instructions For The Offensive. Instructions No. 6	27/07/1917	27/07/1917
Miscellaneous	Time Table Of Attack. To accompany 49th Infantry Brigade Instructions For The Offensive. (Instruction No. 1). Appendix "A"		
Map	15th Division Map No. 2		
Miscellaneous	2nd. R. Irish Regt. 49th. I.R. No. S.C.C. 2/119/1	26/07/1917	26/07/1917
Miscellaneous	49th I.B. No. S.C.C. 2/119	25/07/1917	25/07/1917
Miscellaneous	Notes On The Country North-East Of The Zonnebeke-Staden Line To The Bruges-Ghent Canal	15/07/1917	15/07/1917
Map	Map Showing Woods Streams Etc		
Miscellaneous	90		
Heading	Raid Secret By 49th Infantry Brigade. On Enemy Trenches Between Maedelstede & Peckham		
Miscellaneous	49th Infy Bde. No. B.O. 89/2-12-1-17	12/01/1917	12/01/1917
Operation(al) Order(s)	49th Infantry Brigade Order No. 89-10-1-17	10/01/1917	10/01/1917
Miscellaneous	Preliminary Orders For Raid Appendix. I	03/01/1917	03/01/1917
Miscellaneous	49th Infy Bde No. S.O. 945/1-6-1-17 Appendix I	06/01/1917	06/01/1917
Miscellaneous	49th Infy Bde No. S.O. 945/2-8-1-17	08/01/1917	08/01/1917
Miscellaneous	8th R. Innis. Fus. No. 3/217/1-13/1/17	13/01/1917	13/01/1917
Miscellaneous	Raid by 7/8 R.I.F. 12th Jan 1917	12/01/1917	12/01/1917
Miscellaneous	Preliminary Orders For Raid	03/01/1917	03/01/1917
Miscellaneous	49th Infy Bde. No. S.O. 945/1-6-1-17	06/01/1917	06/01/1917
Miscellaneous	49th Infy Bde. No. S.O. 945/2-8-1-17	08/01/1917	08/01/1917
Miscellaneous	49th Infy Bde. No. B.O. 89-11-1-17	11/01/1917	11/01/1917
Miscellaneous	Scheme For Battalion Raid By 7/8th Royal Irish Fusiliers. Appendix II.		
Map	49th Inf. Bde. 9.1.17		

Miscellaneous	Orders For Raid By Lieut. Colonel. K.C. Weldon/Commanding, 7/8th Royal Irish Fusiliers. Appendix III		
Map	49th Inf. Bde. 3.1.17		
Miscellaneous	Orders For Dummy Raid By O.C. 7th R. Inniskilling Fus. Appendix IV		
Operation(al) Order(s)	16th Divisional Artillery. Operation Order No. 35 Appendix V	08/01/1917	08/01/1917
Miscellaneous	16th D.A. No. R. 2573. 9-1-17 Appendix V	09/01/1917	09/01/1917
Miscellaneous	16th D.A. No. R. 2573/1. 9-1-17 Appendix V	09/01/1917	09/01/1917
Miscellaneous	Scheme For Trench Mortar Bombardments		
Miscellaneous	B. 2nd Trench Mortars. Scheme For Trench Mortar Bombardment		
Miscellaneous	49th Machine Gun Company. Orders For Raid		
Miscellaneous	Signal Communications. Appendix VIII.	09/01/1917	09/01/1917
Miscellaneous	Time Table Appendix IX		
Map	49th Inf. Bde. 9.1.17		
Map	Map. "B2"		
Map	Map "B1"		

1277/4

7/6 Battalion Royal Inniskilling Fusiliers

Sep 1917 — May 1918

16. DIVISION
49 INF BDE

7/8 BN Royal INNISKILLING FUSILIERS

1917 SEP – 1918 MAY

TO 30 DIV 89 BDE

WAR DIARY.

FOR MONTH OF SEPTEMBER, 1917.

VOLUME 1

UNIT:- 7/8th Btn. R. Inniskilling Fuslrs

Army Form C. 2118.

WAR DIARY
or
INTELLIGENCE SUMMARY.
(Erase heading not required.) 7/6 R Innis Killing Fus PAGE 156.

Place	Date 1917	Hour	Summary of Events and Information	Remarks and references to Appendices
ERVILLERS No 5 Camp	Sept 1		Brigade in Div Divisional Reserve.	
"	2		Above the 1st instant Lt Col HN Young 15 D. informed that the 7 Divisional wire was sunk by the division to the 36th Div. Lieut Col HN Young is at present dispersal other Trickery near Reuve were instruction of the 1st in 1/5 Inniskilling & Auth 16 Div A1929	
			d 1/9/17 + 49/15 Inf BM sec/M/506. Trench bombs received & being Iard on South Potion of camp 55 OR's proceeded for attachment to the 174th Tunnelling Coy. A Coy moved into accommodation formed by 2nd R.T. Regt at BEHONCOURT C " " " " 7/6 R Ir Ins " B + D Coys moved " " " " " Twing at the 16th on 1st S side of the road sub. remarked by 16 tents The 6th D.mm.org 7th Rangers 47th Bn moving into the N. of N. staff 7th Camp	

Army Form C. 2118.

WAR DIARY
or
INTELLIGENCE SUMMARY.
(Erase heading not required.)

7/8th R. Inniskilling Fus.

Instructions regarding War Diaries and Intelligence Summaries are contained in F. S. Regs., Part II and the Staff Manual respectively. Title pages will be prepared in manuscript.

Place	Date	Hour	Summary of Events and Information	Remarks and references to Appendices
ERVILLERS CAMP No 5.	Sept 4		No 5 Camp, officially named ENNISKILLEN CAMP.	
	4		MAJOR R. G. KERR assumes command of the Batt. vice Lt. Col. Young.	
	4		Relieve the 9th R. Dublin Fus in Right Support, Dispositions as follows:— Bn. H.Qrs. T.23 c 7.9. (FRANCE sheet 51B) A Coy: St. LEGER. B " T.23 d 8.1 C " T.23 a 5.5 D " QUARRY T.18 7.4.	
	6.		A coy moves to T.29.7.9.	
	10.		Relieve the 2nd R. Irish Reg in the Right Sub Sector. Four coys in the front line, each fusing their own Support line. Coys, U.14 2.8 to LUMP & Ave (exclusive) U.9d 2.8	
	16		Relieved by 9th R. Dub Fus in right Sub sector. The Batt. moves into Bngde Reserve at ENNISKILLEN CAMP (ERVILLERS)	

A6945 Wt. W14921/M1160 350,000 12/16 D.D.&L. Forms/C./2118/14

WAR DIARY
or
INTELLIGENCE SUMMARY.

(Erase heading not required.)

Army Form C. 2118.

7/8th R. Inniskilling Fus.

Place	Date	Hour	Summary of Events and Information	Remarks and references to Appendices
ERVILLERS	16		Remained at ENNISKILLEN CAMP from 16th to 28th SEPT.	
Rt. SUPPORT	28.		The Batt. relieves to 9th R. Dub. Fus. in Right Support.	
			R.J. Kerr, Major	
			Comdg 7/8th R. Inniskilling Fus	
			30th SEPT 1917	

WAR DIARY

FOR MONTH OF OCTOBER, 1917.

UNIT 7/8 Btn R. Inniskilling Fus

VOLUME NUMBER 2

Army Form C. 2118.

WAR DIARY
or
INTELLIGENCE SUMMARY.
(Erase heading not required.)

1/5 R. Innis. Fus.
Page 159

Instructions regarding War Diaries and Intelligence Summaries are contained in F. S. Regs., Part II. and the Staff Manual respectively. Title pages will be prepared in manuscript.

Place	Date	Hour	Summary of Events and Information	Remarks and references to Appendices
R.S. FEET	11th		Batt. still in support to 2nd R. Insk. Regt.	
			Disposition of Coys as under A Coy T.23.d	
			B " T.23.c	
			C " BURREY	
			D " T.23.a	
			HQ T.22.a	
			Day was quiet, work done to improve quarters. Attempts constantly made by Sappers & men of the Royal Engineers	
FRONT LINE	11th		Batt. relieved the 2nd R Insk Regt in the Right hub Sector. V.14.A.2.8 to LOMPLOMS eastward.	
			V.7a.2.5. Disposition of Coys A Coy on right. B Coy in Centre. C Coy left centre D Left	
			Each Coy finding its own support	
			Lt. Col A.J Walkey M.C. returns from Leave and took over command of Batt. from	
			Major R.G Kerr M.C.	
			The line was fairly quiet, enemy heavy trench mortars did considerable damage to	

WAR DIARY
or
INTELLIGENCE SUMMARY.
(Erase heading not required.)

Army Form C. 2118.

7/8 R Inns Ds   page 160

Instructions regarding War Diaries and Intelligence Summaries are contained in F. S. Regs., Part II, and the Staff Manual respectively. Title pages will be prepared in manuscript.

Place	Date	Hour	Summary of Events and Information	Remarks and references to Appendices
Front Line H.Qts	5/6		From right by the trenches were badly damaged and numerous casualties were suffered. A Counter attack about was carried out in severe hand to hand to hand fighting from our front line at 7pm which appeared to be highly successful. The second shoot always to 6am h'but also held place owing to unfavorable weather conditions. The Huns were shelling our trenches practice Barrage on enemy trenches at 6pm.	
	7/6		(a) 26.80 L Zero Barrage enemy front line from (f) plus 5" minutes plus to 30 L 2/Lt 96.90. (b) Zero plus 5 mins Lift layer about 2 mins L Zero plus 10 mins. Inflame TUNNEL TREACH from L Zero plus 13 mins V.1d a 22.62 L F.18 74.64 Enemy hitting heavy, medium and light trench Mortars and Machine Guns all Co-operates	

Army Form C. 2118.

WAR DIARY
or
INTELLIGENCE SUMMARY.
(Erase heading not required.)

Place	Date	Hour	Summary of Events and Information	Remarks and references to Appendices
FROMILLON	7/Oct	12 w/p	Heavy returns. Light trench mortars shot in enemy wire and narrow trenches	
		1.30p		
	9/Oct		Enemy trench mortars still carrying active on our Right Coy front	
	10/Oct		Battn was relieved by 9th Bn R. Dublin Fusiliers and moved back to ENNISKILLEN CAMP	
ENNISKILLEN	11/Oct		ERVILLERS	
CAMP	"		Platoon + Coy training was carried out across his town. 'A' Coy carried off all	
	22/Oct		audies + prizes and practice in preparation in preparation in enemy trenches	
			The Camp was generally improved. Fireplaces built into huts and fuel in fact	
			plate of iron. A large hut was obtained and erected to be used as a	
			recreation room + canteen for the Batn.	
Right Support	23rd Oct	2pm	The Battn relieved the 9th R. Dublin Fus in Right Support disposition	
			A Coy T.23.a D Coy T.23.a	C Coy remained at ENNISKILLEN CAMP to practice
			B " QUARRY H.Q. T.22.d	raid scheme

Army Form C. 2118.

WAR DIARY
or
INTELLIGENCE SUMMARY.
(Erase heading not required.)

Instructions regarding War Diaries and Intelligence Summaries are contained in F. S. Regs., Part II. and the Staff Manual respectively. Title pages will be prepared in manuscript.

page 162

Place	Date	Hour	Summary of Events and Information	Remarks and references to Appendices
Right Support	22/64 to 28/64		Worked on Coy positions under direction of R.E.'s was a carrying and wiring parties. Parties were provided for the FRONT LINE	
FRONT LINE	28/64	3pm	The Batt relieved the 2"R Scots Regt in FRONT LINE. 2 Coys holding the FRONT LINE as follows: A Coy V.14.a.2.8 to W.13/2 (inclusive) B. W.13/2 to PLUM LANE D. PLUM LANE to 07.x.2.8. 2 Coys in LINCOLN SUPPORT.	
	29/64	12.30pm to 1.30pm	Enemy shewing intention fight French trying carried out a shed on enemy lines and various lengths, our battling and M.B. Co-operate	
		10.45pm	Raid was carried out on enemy trenches. Operation Item and Repot attached as Appendices A. B. The rest of the time passed very quietly.	

WAR DIARY or INTELLIGENCE SUMMARY

Army Form C. 2118.

7/8 R. Innis. Fus.

PAGE 113

Place	Date	Hour	Summary of Events and Information	Remarks and references to Appendices
			Officers rejoining during month	
	1/Oct		Capt Lord F.J.M.D. DUNSANY	
	2"		Lt. Col. A.J. MALKEY M.C. took over Command on 4/10/17	
	3"		2/Lt G.L. WILLIAMS	
	9"		2/Lt H.P.H. MONTGOMERY	
	27"		2/Lt T.J. STACK	
			Officers Quitting	
	2 Oct		Lt. QM. G. SEARLE left 8" Army to 225th Reserve Batn of Inf. COLCHESTER	
	9 Oct		Lt. H.V. LOWRY to hospital	
	12"		Lt. F. O'NEILL to TMBS	
	19"		Major H.M. BIDDULPH to 16.IBD	
	27"		2/Lt W.H. BROWNE to TMBS	
	27"		2/Lt H.P.H. MONTA went temporarily attached 7/8 R Innis Brs.	
	29"		2/Lt R.F. CASEY to R.F.C. reserve	

Army Form C. 2118.

WAR DIARY
or
INTELLIGENCE SUMMARY.
(Erase heading not required.)

7/8 R. Innis. Fus. PAGE No. 4.

Place	Date	Hour	Summary of Events and Information	Remarks and references to Appendices
	29th		Officer casualties.	
			2/Lt F.D. Murphy M.C. wounded at duty evacuated to hospital 30-10-17	
			OTHER RANKS	
			KILLED 4	
			DIED of WOUNDS 1	
			WOUNDED 17	
			~~Shell Shock~~ =	
			" and MISSING 1	
			MISSING 1	

C J Watkins Col
Comdg 7/8 R Innis Fus
2/11/17

APPENDIX "A"

SECRET.   Copy No. 8

49th Infantry Brigade Order. No. 173.

Oct. 27th, 1917.

Ref. Map CHERISY
   Edn. 3C, 1/10,000.

1.   A raid will be carried out on the 29th October, 1917 by a Company 7/8th R. Innis Fus. (Strength of Raiding Party about 4 Officers and 100 Other Ranks.)
   O.C. Raid Captain H.A. GREEN, M.C.

   VI Corps Heavy Artillery, 16th Div. Artillery, 49th T.M.Battery, 49th M.G.Company and No. 3 Special Company, R.E. are co-operating.

   The 47th Inf. Bde. on the right, and the 153rd Inf. Bde. on the left are making demonstrations.

2.   OBJECT.

   To obtain sufficient prisoners for identification purposes and for information, and to inflict damage upon enemy personnel and defences.

3.   RAID AREA.

   Trenches to be raided are - Enemy front line and saps from U.7.d.55.85 to U.7.d.70.40 and Support Line about 120 yards in rear of above and two communication trenches connecting front line and support.

4.   ASSEMBLY POSITIONS.

   British Front Line from U.7.d.35.75 to U.7.d.35.40.

5.   TASKS.

   Raid Company will be devided into 4 parties whose tasks are allotted as follows :-

No. 1. Deal with OLDENBURG LANE from front line to support, picketing trench junctions at U.7.d. 75.85 and U.7.d.85.85 and working South along TUNNEL SUPPORT.

No. 2. Front line from U.7.d.60.80 to U.7.d.65.65. Special squads to be told off to deal with deep dugouts and prisoners. Tunnel entrances will be dealt with by smoke bombs at alternate entrances, the others being left as "bolt-holes".

No. 3. Deal with sap and communication trench on South of raid front. Work North along TUNNEL SUPPORT, picketing junction at U.7.d.90.60. One squad of this party will proceed direct to bomb saphead at U.7.d.50.40.

No. 4. Front line from U.7.d.65.65 to U.7.d.70.40. Special Squads to deal with deep dugouts, (as for No. 2 party) and prisoners.

   A covering party of one Lewis Gun and a squad of bombers will protect each flank of the raiding party.

6. ARTILLERY. 18-pdrs.

Zero to Zero plus 2 minutes - Intense barrage on front line from U.7.b.7.7. - U.7.b.4.1. - U.7.d.7.4.

Zero plus 2 minutes - Lift to TUNNEL SUPPORT firing on that trench until Zero plus 5 minutes.

Zero plus 5 minutes and onwards - lift from TUNNEL SUPPORT and form Box Barrage along lines U.7.b.5.0 - U.8.a.1.1 - U.8.c.2.4 - U.7.d.7.3.

Fire will cease at Zero plus 45 minutes, unless artillery are notified to the contrary.

4.5" Howitzers.

Commencing at Zero :-

Two Hows. On trench junctions at U.7.b.7.4, afterwards searching up along trenches running North and North East from this point.
One How. OLDENBURG LANE at U.8.a.3.3.
Two Hows. CEYLON TRENCH U.8.a.4.3 and U.8.a.7.0.
One How. One U.8.c.4.0.

7. TRENCH MORTARS.

2" Mortars.

Commencing at Zero :-

One Mortar on Sap and MEBU at U.14.a.1.7 (JUNO).
One Mortar on MEBU at U.7.d.7.3. (FLORA).
One Mortar U.13.b.25.20.
One Mortar on MEBU at U.14.a.4.7. (MINERVA).

3" Stokes Guns.

4 guns Zero to Zero plus 1 minute - Intense barrage on front line U.7.b.7.3 - U.7.b.4.1. - U.7.d.7.4. *to plus 2 mins*
Zero plus 1 minute *2* guns firing on frontage U.7.b.5.0 - U.7.d.7.3. ~~Cease fire.~~ *lift on to Tunnell Support*

2 guns. Traverse enemy front line South of raid front from zero onwards.

4" Stokes Guns.

Will, if wind is favourable, at Zero, form a Smoke Barrage on flanks and support line of raid front.

8. No. 3 SPECIAL COMPANY, R.E.

No. 3 Special Coy, R.E., should the wind be favourable, are co-operating by forming a Smoke Barrage on either flank.

Targets.

1. U.7.b.5.0 to U.7.b.9.1. - 3 guns.
2. U.7.d.7.3 to U.8.c.1.5. - 3 guns.
3. U.8.c.10.50 to U.8.a.1.1. - 4 guns.

9. MACHINE GUNS.

(a) Zero to zero plus 8 minutes – enfilade TUNNEL SUPPORT TRENCH. in U.7.d.
(b) Barrage along general line U.7.b.7.9 – U.8.central.
(c) Sunken Road in U.8.a. and c.
(d) Fire also on U.7.b.4.1, FONTAINE, REBUS JUNO and organised shell holes about U.14.a.9.7.
(e) Enfilade PAG ALLEY.
(f) Search SENSEE VALLEY in U.7.b.
(g) Arrange with Division on right to enfilade SUNKEN ROAD in U.14.b and d and TUNNEL TRENCH in U.14.d. and U.20.b.

LEWIS GUNS.

Lewis Guns to fire short bursts at intervals along enemy front line South of Raid Front.

10. WIRE CUTTING.

Artillery and T.M's to cut wire on raid front, and also at other selected places in order to avoid raising suspicion. Gaps to be kept open by Lewis Gun fire at night.

11. DIVISION ON LEFT.

The 51st Division on the left are arranging to put down at Zero a Barrage of H.E. and Smoke on the German front line in U.1.b. which will lift to the enemy support line.

In conjunction with this, the 7th (S.I.H) R. Irish Regt., if wind is favourable, will throw out some "P" Bombs at end of PUG LANE, and open fire with Lewis Guns, in direction of FONTAINE.

47th Inf. Bde. will co-operate by making a feint attack against the right about U.14.d.1.4 to U.20.b.4.7 by putting down a barrage of Stokes Guns and Lewis Guns, and if wind is favourable using smoke and "P" Bombs.

12. RAID HEADQUARTERS.

Headquarters of O.C. Raid will be in deep dugout at U.7.d.10.20. All reports will be sent here and on return raiding party will assemble in this dugout. Prisoners and captured material will be sent to Right Battalion headquarters.

13. SIGNALS.

The Signalling Officer, 7/8th R. Innis Fus. will arrange for direct communication by telephone and runners between Battalion H.Q. and H.Q. of O.C. Raid. All lines will be left as clear as possible for raid messages.

The Recall Signal will be GOLDEN RAIN ROCKETS fired some distance behind our front line.

14. TRAFFIC.

JANET AVENUE, CHERRY, PEAR and PLUMB LANES will be kept clear of all traffic except that which concerns the raid, also BURG SUPPORT between CHERRY and PLUMB LANES.

15. MEDICAL.

The Medical Officer will establish an Adv. Aid Post in deep dugout at U.7.d.15.20 where stretcher cases will be dealt with. Walking wounded will proceed via JANET AVENUE direct to AID POST in QUARRY, first reporting to a N.C.O. who will be posted at junction of JANET AVENUE and BURG SUPPORT.

16. Watches will be synchronized at 12 noon and 2 p.m. at Brigade H.Q. Representatives of following will attend at these times :-

    Divisional Machine Guns.
    7th (S.I.H) R. Irish Regt.
    7/8th R. Innis Fus.
    D.T.M.O.
    49th T.M.Battery.
    16th Div. Artillery.
    No. 3 Special Coy, R.E.
    and South I. Horse

17. 7/8th R. Innis Fus. will reduce their trench garrison to a minimum. As many men as possible will be accommodated in dugouts.

18. LUMP LANE will be cleared, in small parties and silently, at Zero minus 20, and regarrisoned when the situation quietens down.

19. Zero hour will be notified later.

20. ACKNOWLEDGE.

                                    T.W. MacDonald   Captain,

              Brigade Major, 49th Infantry Brigade.

Issued through Signals.

        Copy No. 1 to G.O.C.
            ,,   2   Staff Captain.
            ,,   3   Bde. Intelligence Officer.
            ,,   4   Bde. Signal Officer.
            ,,   5   2nd R. Irish Regt.
            ,,   6   7th (S.I.H) R. Irish Regt.
            ,,   7   7/8th R. Innis Fus.
            ,,   8   7/8th R. Innis Fus.
            ,,   9   7/8th R. Irish Fus.
            ,, 10   49th M.G. Company.
            ,, 11   49th T.M.Battery.
            ,, 12   No. 3 Special Coy, R.E.
            ,, 13   D.T.M.O.
            ,, 14   D.M.G.O.
            ,, 15   16th Div. Arty.
            ,, 16   16th Div. (G).
            ,, 17   47th Inf. Bde.
            ,, 18   48th Inf. Bde.
            ,, 19   153rd Inf. Bde.
            ,, 20   180th Bde. R.F.A.
            ,, 21   155th Field Coy, R.E.
            ,, 22   157th Field Coy, R.E.
            ,, 23-24 War Diary.
            ,, 25   File.
            ,, 26   *VI" Corps H.A.*

Artillery & T.M. Barrage Map

49th Inf. Bde Raid.

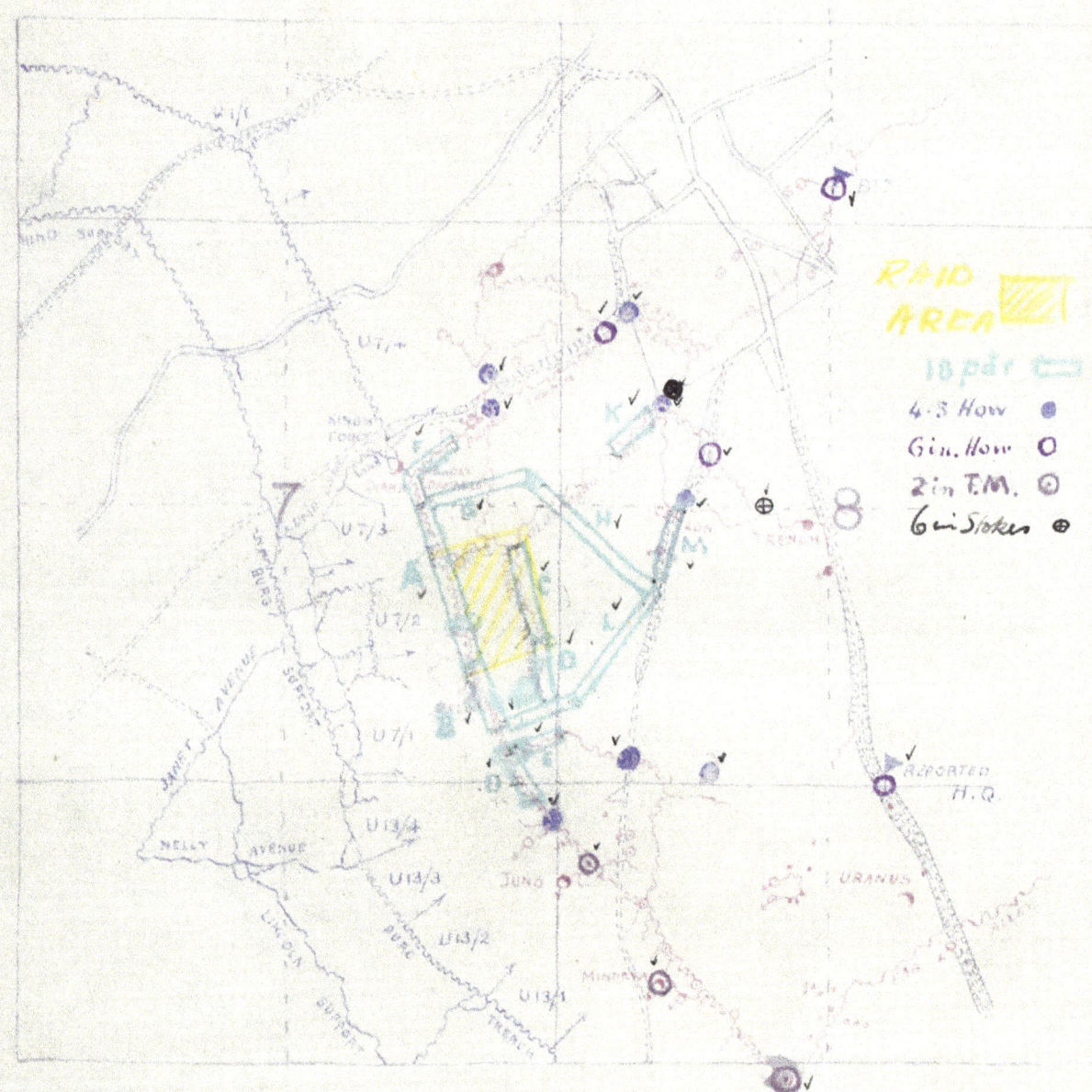

APPENDIX "B"

All recipients of 49th Inf. Bde.
Order No. 173.

49th Inf. Bde. No. B.C. 173/2 - 30-10-17.

The following account of a raid carried out by one Company, 7/8th R. Innis Fus. on the evening of October 29th is forwarded for your information.

The enemy trenches were entered on a front of 220 yards to a depth of 150 yards:-

TIME TABLE.

4.45 p.m.	Barrage commenced: all started precisely to time.
4.50 p.m.	O.C. Raid reported all went over well, and none fell.
5 p.m.	Reported got into enemy's line without opposition.
5.15 p.m.	2 prisoners reported, and our men had started to return. Recall signal sent up.
5.30 p.m.	Report "all in" received. Barrage ceased. 1 wounded prisoner reported.

INFORMATION.

Barrage: All are unanimous in stating that this was excellent.

Wire: Our gaps were adequate and caused no delay to raiders. Enemy wire cut to pieces, and presented no obstacle. Sap HOLE LANE easily entered.

State of enemy trenches: Very bad indeed; no duckboards except outside Tunnel entrances. It is hard to state measurements, as trenches are so knocked about, but on an average, they are about 6 or 7 feet deep, about 4 yards wide at top and afford no cover. These remarks apply to C.T's as well as front line and support. The last named being in such a wretched condition that it was hard to discern where exactly it ran. There were no firesteps worth mentioning, but there were several short saps and T heads running out both front and rear from front line.

DUGOUTS AND TUNNEL ENTRANCES.

4 dugouts of sorts in TUNNEL SUPPORT. No dugouts in OLDENBURG LANE between front line and support. 9 entrances to tunnel in front line (apparently all led into tunnel). about 20 yards apart. First six yards down entrance had no steps and there appeared to be a steel door a short distance down which prevented us bombing or smoking the enemy out, although he dived for these entrances.

Both officers of front line parties agree about these doors, and Lieut. ARMSTRONG went down and tried to open one but failed. There is a recess in the trench each side of entrance with a steel loophole. Bombs are also stored beside these recesses.

SAP - HOLE LANE.

About 6 feet deep at front line - gradually decreasing to 4 feet near head where a pit is dug. Enemy bombed and sniped from here at first; there appeared to be about 20 Bosche in the sap and some of these had emerged from dugouts. After sap party had gone down to front line. A second party of ours bombed these from the top, but it was difficult to see what happened as sap was full of smoke and flame

2.

There is a listening post or M.G. emplacement about 40 yards from front line opposite OLDENBURG LANE; it has an elbow rest and there were about a dozen bombs there.

There is a C.T. from support to front line just S. of OLDENBURG LANE; it is called LIEBEN GRABEN.

M.G's, T.M's, etc.

There was some M.G. fire, but it was mostly over heads of raiders, some of it from right flank, and some from in rear of support line. No M.G's or T.M's were seen.

There were 4 steel dummies looking over parapet near MOLE LANE.

HOLDING OF LINE.

Most of the enemy were encountered in MOLE LANE and near it. Our 2 Northern parties saw only about 6 Bosche between them. Many of the enemy either had their gas masks on, or were putting them on.

ENEMY BARRAGE. - was put down at Zero plus 3 minutes along LINCOLN SUPPORT, JANET AVENUE and NELLY AVENUE - mostly 4.2's. He also put down a barrage just in front of our wire. Some incendiary shells used.

LIGHTS. Golden Rain and Very Lights sent up from flanks. Little damage was done by enemy fire.

OUR CASUALTIES.

2/Lieut Morphy, M.C. Right hand burned rather badly by incendiary shell.
9 O.R. wounded (most of them only slightly).
None killed or missing.

DAMAGE TO ENEMY.

From careful enquiries, it is estimated that 27 were killed, and at least 10 wounded. 3 prisoners, 1 badly wounded, 1 slightly and 1 unwounded.
12 or 14 bomb stores blown up by Mills Bombs.

GENERAL.

Officers and N.C.O's state that the trenches are in such a bad state that they are practically untenable.
The enemy had no fight in him after he had thrown a few bombs, and the raiders regard the affair as a "soft thing".

(sd) A.J.WALKEY, Lieut Colonel,

Commanding 9/8th R. Innis Fus.

WAR DIARY

FOR MONTH OF NOVEMBER, 1917.

VOLUME:- 3

UNIT:- 7th/8th Ro. Inniskilling Fus.

Army Form C. 2118.

WAR DIARY
or
INTELLIGENCE SUMMARY.
(Erase heading not required.)

7/8 R. INNIS. FUS.   Page 15fl

Instructions regarding War Diaries and Intelligence Summaries are contained in F. S. Regs., Part II. and the Staff Manual respectively. Title pages will be prepared in manuscript.

Place	Date	Hour	Summary of Events and Information	Remarks and references to Appendices
ENNISKILLEN	1 Nov		Were relieved in FRONT LINE by 2nd Bn. R. Dublin Fus. and Batt. moved to	
CAMP.	Nov 1st		ENNISKILLEN CAMP.	
	2		Remained in ENNISKILLEN CAMP Resting and refitting	
	Nov 3		Relieved the 1st R. Dublin Fus. in FRONT LINE. RIGHT SUB SECTION V.14 & 2 R. LUTTLAINE	
			on sheet V.28.2.E.	
			Disposition of Coys "A" Right	
			B. Right Centre	
			C. Left Centre } Each Coy found its own Support	
			D. Left	
	Nov 5		From 2.0pm to 2.45pm Wd HEAVY. MEDIUM and LIGHT T.M. in conjunction with Aeroplanes	
			Artillery Carried out a successful shoot on enemy trenches	
	Nov 4		At 5.2pm the Div Howitzers carried out successful gas bombardment of Sunken Rd in V.15a.	

Army Form C. 2118.

WAR DIARY
or
INTELLIGENCE SUMMARY.
(Erase heading not required.)

7th R. Innis. Fus.   Page 165

Place	Date	Hour	Summary of Events and Information	Remarks and references to Appendices
FRONT LINE	Nov 15	12pm	The TMB's and Div Artillery again carried out a programme of wire cutting on enemy dugouts.	
		1.5pm		
	Nov 7		A third TMB shoot again successful.	
			During the whole time the Heavy Batteries were engaged on wire cutting and shoots on MEBU's in enemy front line system. Their shooting was visibly a constant source of the front line, but only a very few shells fell short.	
			The enemy were fairly quiet. He scarcely retaliated for our previous bombardments but he shot some Heavy Trench Mortars onto TOMBST AVE. which he damaged in several places.	
	Nov 8		The Batt. was relieved in FRONT LINE by the following Batt⁻	
			Right 10th R. Dublin Fus
			Right Centre 2nd R. Dublin Fus
			Left Centre 2nd R. Irish Regt. The Batt. moved back to BELFAST CAMP ERVILLERS.
			Left 7th R. Irish Fus.	

Army Form C. 2118.

WAR DIARY
or
INTELLIGENCE SUMMARY.
(Erase heading not required.)

7/8 R Innis. Fus from 16 C.

Place	Date	Hour	Summary of Events and Information	Remarks and references to Appendices
SUPPORT	Nov 19		The Battn moved up into assembly positions. Two platoons were attached to 2°R Irish Rifles. 1 platoon to 7/8 R Irish Fus, 1 platoon to 49" Machine Gun Company.	
			Disposition as under, 'A' Coy SUNKEN Rd. T.17.a	
			'B' " SUNKEN Rd T.22.a	
			'C' " SUNKEN Rd T.22.a with Coy HQ and 1 platoon at T.23.c.2.9	
			'D' " QUARRY with 1 platoon in BURG SUPPORT V.7d.1.3	
			1 platoon at V.7c.b.2.	
			This was SUPPORT for the attack on enemy FRONT LINE SYSTEM	
	Nov 20	6.20am	The Division attacked at 6.20 am. 'A' Coy moved from T.17.a and was attached to the	
		5.30pm	7/8 R Irish Fus at 5.30pm	
	Nov 21		The Battn relieved the 7/8 R Irish Fus in the captured enemy trenches, centre sub-section, V.7d. H5.15 to V.7a.90.75. Disposition FRONT LINE. 'C' Coy on RIGHT	
			'D' " LEFT.	
			'B' Coy in Support V.7c.90.90.	
			Disposition of Support Coys A. in Dugouts V.7d. 30.25.	
			V.7a.1.3	

Army Form C. 2118.

WAR DIARY
or
INTELLIGENCE SUMMARY.
(Erase heading not required.)

7/8 Bn. R. Innis. Fus.   page 166

Place	Date	Hour	Summary of Events and Information	Remarks and references to Appendices
FRONT LINE	Nov 21"		The line was very quiet, the enemy shot our front line with T.M's. Little damage was done.	
	24.		On night of 23"/24" at 7.0pm the S.O.S was sent up from FRONT LINE but no attack developed.	
	Nov 25"		The enemy only layed down a barrage. All was normal by 8.30pm.	
	Nov 26"		The Batt" was relieved the 2". R. Irish Regt. in the RIGHT Sub-section by bringing up Echelons 'B' and placing it "X" Coy under Command of MAJOR R.G. WEAR M.C.	
			The Batt" Front was handed over to V.8.C. 1.2.	
ENNISKILLEN	Nov 28"		The Batt" was relieved by the 2". R. Dublin Fus. and moved back to ENNISKILLEN CAMP.	
CAMP	Nov 30"		The days spent in west were devoted to thorough cleaning and refitting of Batt. Instruction in light German Machine Gun 08/15 pattern and general training. The Batt" relieved the 10". R. Dublin Fus. in SUPPORT dispositions.	
			A Coy SUNKEN Rd T.23 a. Batt. HA SUNKEN Rd T.22 d. 8.9.	
			B " SUNKEN Rd T.23 c.	
			C " SUNKEN Rd T.23 d. (Two Platoons and two platoons at T.22 d.9.9.	
			D " SUNKEN Rd T.17 a.	

3/12/17   G. Walkuff Col.
Comnd'g 7/8th R. Innis. Fus.

Army Form C. 2118.

WAR DIARY
or
INTELLIGENCE SUMMARY.
(Erase heading not required.)

7/6 Bn. R. Innis. Fus. page 167

Instructions regarding War Diaries and Intelligence Summaries are contained in F. S. Regs., Part II. and the Staff Manual respectively. Title pages will be prepared in manuscript.

Place	Date	Hour	Summary of Events and Information	Remarks and references to Appendices
			OFFICERS JOINING	
	Nov 1		MAJOR V.H. PARR DSO M.C.	
	"17	2/Lt	W.J. LAVELLE	
	"17	2/Lt	T.J. JOHNSTON	
	"17	2/Lt	E. ILLINGWORTH	
	"8	2/Lt	S. PRESTON	
	"24	2/Lt	H. HOBSON	
	"24	2/Lt	W.A. WILKINSON	
	"24	2/Lt	H.G. LACEY	
			OFFICERS QUITTING	
	Nov 12		Lt.Col. H.N. YOUNG D.S.O. (returned to England) W.o. A/6 Adv. HQ A/29/1 (a.1) d 30/9/17	
	"20	2/Lt	LILLEY to hospital	
	"20	2/Lt	G.L. WILLIAMS wounded 16 Bn. A/57/75 d 25/4/17. Sec. W/gs d 27/4/17	
	"20	Lt	A.H.H. ARMSTRONG to R.F.C.	
	"23	Capt.	A.E.C. TRIMBLE wounded	

Army Form C. 2118.

WAR DIARY
or
INTELLIGENCE SUMMARY.
(Erase heading not required.)

7/8 Bn. R. Innis. Fus. page 168

Place	Date	Hour	Summary of Events and Information	Remarks and references to Appendices
	Nov 2		OFFICERS QUITTING B	
			2/Lt. E. ILLINGWORTH to hospital.	
			HONOURS & AWARDS	
			The un-mentioned have been awarded decorations.	
			MILITARY CROSS	
			Capt. A.E.C. TRIMBLE wounded in action 22.11.17	
			2/Lt. G.L. WILLIAMS do 20.11.17	
			Lt. T.R. MULREY	
			Lt. A.H.H. ARMSTRONG	
			DCM	
			23231 Sgt GARRY J.C.	
			MM	
			CASUALTIES :- OFFICERS	
			KILLED IN ACTION. 7	
			WOUNDED IN ACTION 35	
			20496 Sgt BRADLEY J.J.	
			21674 " TAYLOR J.	
			20654 " KING G.	
			1876 " MORRIS T.J.	
			25877 Pte McQUADE P.	
			48890 A/C DUNSFORD R.H.	
			JWWalker Lt Col	
			3/12/17 Commdg. 7/8th R. Innis. Fus	

WAR DIARY

FOR MONTH OF DECEMBER, 1917.

VOLUME :- 4

UNIT :- 7/8th Enniskilling Fusiliers

Army Form C. 2118.

WAR DIARY, DECEMBER 1917.
INTELLIGENCE SUMMARY.
(Erase heading not required.)

1/8th R. Inniskilling Fus   Page 169

Instructions regarding War Diaries and Intelligence Summaries are contained in F. S. Regs., Part II, and the Staff Manual respectively. Title pages will be prepared in manuscript.

Place	Date 1917	Hour	Summary of Events and Information	Remarks and references to Appendices
CROISILLES SECTOR SUPPORT	Dec 1		In Support, dispositions as shown on page 166. (Not.) Received Warning Order stating that 16th Division (less Artillery) was to be relieved at once by 40th Division.	ag/W
Do	2	5.0 pm	Battalion was relieved by 131th Yorks, on completion of relief moved to	ag/W
FAVILLERS	3	1.0 pm	ENNISKILLEN CAMP, where it was in Divisional Reserve.	
		10.0 pm	The 49th Inf. Bde. moved by march route to BARASTRE AREA (near BAPAUME)	ag/W
BARASTRE		2 pm	The Battn. arrived in Huttments at Afour & bivouacked there until 5th Dec.	ag/W
	5	9.30 am	49th Inf. Bde. moved by march route to TINCOURT AREA & the Battn. arrived in	
BUIRE		6 pm	billets at BUIRE at 6 pm.	ag/W
	6	3 pm	The 49th Inf. Bde. moved to STE. EMELIE , & Coys with support 1st 45th Inf Bde, which had relieved portion of 53rd Division in the Line. The Battn. entrained at	ag/W
		5 pm	HAMEL at 3/pm & arrived in billets in STE. EMELIE at 5/pm.	
STE EMELIE	6/12		Bde. in support. For two nights the whole Battn. was employed in digging a new front (MULE TRENCH) S. of PRIEL CUTTING. One third of the Battn. lived in barracks during time in Support. STE EMILIE was frequently shelled, on one occasion a direct hit was obtained by a 4.2 shell on a hut containing about 40 O.R. Six were wounded, two dying subsequently.	ag/W

WAR DIARY or INTELLIGENCE SUMMARY

Army Form C. 2118.

December 1917   1/8th R. Innis. Div.   Page 170

Place	Date 1917	Hour	Summary of Events and Information	Remarks and references to Appendices
STE EMELIE	10/12	4.0pm	Batt. marched out to relieve 2nd K.S.L.I. in front line in charge of 74th (S.H.)	
			R.S. bef. in front line from No.13 Copse to F11 a 8.6	
FRONT		9.0pm	On completion of relief, dispositions were as follows:	
LINE			D. Coy. Nos 12 & 13 Coys PRIEL CUTTING & MULE TRENCH	
			B " CRUCIFORM POST, 2 Platoons HEYTHROP LANE 1 Platoon	
			BIRD LANE " "	
			A " HEYTHROP POST B. Coy. GRAFTON POST	
			Advanced Bn HQ, F 4 (central) Bn HQ F 10 c 4.4	
			Vicinity of Bn HQ was shelled during relief + casualties occurred	
	11/12		Holding front line as above. The line was fairly quiet except for intermittent shelling - mainly on left coy. Bn HQ & neighbour hood	
		at 3.30am	16 enemy carried out a heavy bombardment on MULE TRENCH & PRIEL CUTTING. The fire lasted 20 minutes + no infantry action resulted + little damage was done.	
	12/12		On the morning of the 12th, we recaptured an enemy German prisoner at the eastern end of PRIEL CUTTING.	

WAR DIARY or INTELLIGENCE SUMMARY

Army Form C. 2118.

December 1917

(Erase heading not required.)

Place	Date 1917	Hour	Summary of Events and Information	Remarks and references to Appendices
FRONT LINE	Dec 17	9/am	The 1/8th Inf Bn relieved through Hingh. Inf Bn. The 2nd R Dublin Fus. relieved the Battn which on completion of relief marches to STE EMILIE & entrained for HAMEL arriving there at 11.30 pm & marching to billets in TINCOURT, where the Battn was in Divisional Reserve.	appx
"	17/22		During the time no training was carried out & men occupied their time in thoroughly cleaning up & refreshing their kits.	appx
LEMPIRE DEFENCES	23	4pm	Entrained at HAMEL, detrained at STE EMILIE at 5.0pm. The 1/8th Inf Rif Btn relieved the 1/8th Inf Btn in right sector the Battn relieved 1st R Munster Fus in LEMPIRE DEFENCES. Dispositions as follows:—	
			A Coy. LEMPIRE WEST OF BASSE BOULOGNE	
			B " LEMPIRE	
	24/29		D " LEMPIRE ROAD	
			C " RONSSOY Bn HQ. F21c 8.4.	
			Work was carried out in wiring strong points & improving comm lines. The two wiring parties of 11/2 pltn were nightly employed on wiring of LEMPIRE WEST wire which held for second time for hours which occurred	appx

WAR DIARY or **INTELLIGENCE SUMMARY.**
(Erase heading not required.)

Army Form C. 2118.

December 1917 1/5th A. Service Bn page 192

Place	Date 1917	Hour	Summary of Events and Information	Remarks and references to Appendices
LE MAIRE				
DEFENCES	Nov 29	9.30a	Above 2nd R.B. Relf in front line, right subsection Dispositions	
FRONT LINE			C Coy Left Post F.15.a.9.6 — F.15.c.9.8	
			A " Right " F.15.c.9.5 — F.24.a.9.0	
			B " Support Dugout Post & QUEUCHETTES WOOD	
			D " KEN LANE	
			(Bn.H.Q.)	GW
	29/31		Both { day as above, Little hostile artillery	
			{ night " " " " "	
			Casualties during month 2 OR killed, 3 OR died of Wounds, 11 OR wounded, 1 OR Missing.	
			Officers joining: Major A.J.M. GORDON, bn from Service Bn 28/12/17	
			" departing: 2nd Lt H. HULEY to England, sick 10.12.17	
			Capt A.A. SEWARD to be employed on Labour	
			Duties Lt I.K. CLARKE to R.F.C 14.12.17	
			Honours & Awards Nº 26160 Sgt T. ROBEY (although 1M.M.) } MILITARY MEDALS	
			34550 L/Cpl E. KNEEBONE }	
			27612 Pte J. FLYNN }	
			3/1/18	GW

Army Form C. 2118.

WAR DIARY
or
INTELLIGENCE SUMMARY.
(Erase heading not required.)

JANUARY 1918.
1/6 R. INNIS. FUS.   Page 1

Place	Date	Hour	Summary of Events and Information	Remarks and references to Appendices
FRONT LINE	1 JAN	to 4 PM	Batt. held the RIGHT SUB SECTION of RIGHT SECTOR of the Divisional Front. being relieved on 7th inst. by the 1st Batt. R. Dublin Fus. marching on completion of relieve to billets in Divisional Reserve at VILLERS FAUCON.	
VILLERS-FAUCON	7 JAN to 9 JAN		Batt. was resting, training and generally cleaning up. Enemy aircraft active almost bombing the neighbourhood. but no casualties suffered. L/Guns were ordered to be lookout guard in Divisional area for anti aircraft work. Several targets were presented and engaged	
GENEVE	9 JAN to 31st		Batt. moved into BRIGADE RESERVE at GENEVE. Relieving 1st Bn. R. MUNSTER FUS. Hd. at E24 A.A.6. A/B Coys in Rly Cutting E24A+7 C&D Coy in Rly Cutting E23 6.84 The time was spent in improving the huts, harness specialist and anti-aircraft L/Guns had considerable work and accidents in army of B.A. Ack has passed over our Front Line System	

WAR DIARY
or
INTELLIGENCE SUMMARY.
(Erase heading not required.)

Army Form C. 2118.

JANUARY 1918.

7/8 R Innis Fus

Page 2

Place	Date	Hour	Summary of Events and Information	Remarks and references to Appendices
FRONT LINE	JAN 16"		The Batt relieved the 7:(S.I.R.) R IRISH REGT in the R SUB-SECTION LEFT SECTOR. HQrs Fin Club A Coy GRAFTON POST. 'B' Coy Support SANDBAGALLEY 'C' Coy Support NEST 1/16 and	
	16/17		D Coy HEYTHROP POST and HEYTHROP LANE	
			ZEBRA POSTS.	
	17"	3.50pm	The enemy put down a very heavy barrage on HEYTHROP POST, and a party of the enemy about 100 strong came over and entered our trench in two places. They 6 min later the remainder beat them off. We suffered a few casualties. 1 off Killed, 7 wounded 7 missing. The whole enterprise finished at 4.10pm. 1 Platoon of C Coy moved forward and reinforced D Coy.	
	18"		B.C. Coys relieved A and D Coys respectively.	
	20"		1 platoon of 'A' Coy moved into HEYTHROP POST, relieving 1 platoon of 'C' Coy who moved to SUPPORT in the NEST.	
	22"		The Batt was relieved in the line by 7:(S.I.R) R Inns. Ryfs. in Amykam of 11th Batt moved to Bde SUPPORT on LEMPIRE — EPEHY RIDGE.	

RNelson Major
3/1/16

WAR DIARY
or
INTELLIGENCE SUMMARY.
(Erase heading not required.)

JANUARY 1918   Army Form C. 2118.
7/8 R. INNIS FUS   Page 3

Place	Date	Hour	Summary of Events and Information	Remarks and references to Appendices
SUPPORT	JAN 22"		The town & the Front Line was one of extremely hard work and also careful	
			The trenches had collapsed in many places owing to the sudden thaw and	
			every trench had as a minimum 2ft of which began mud which was	
			absolutely impassable. Duckboards and roads to the Front Line were used by everyone	
			the enemy also.	
	JAN 23 " 28		The Bat was in SUPPORT disposition :- Bn.HQ F15.6.1.3. and Coy in Cattay	
			at F.2.C. C. Coy. MALASSISE FM. B. Coy. LEMPIRE VILLAGE	
			The town was above 60 level & working parties w/ the main line of	
			resistance were improved and worked on under the supervision of the coys.	
			Pioneer Batt.	
FRONT LINE	JAN 28		Batt relieved the 7"(Sn) R. Irish Rgt. in FRONT LINE disposition.	
			Bn.HQ F10.C.4.6. A.Coy HETHROP POST and Lot ne. B. Coy GRAFTON POST	
			C.Coy NEST YORK ZEBRA POSTS. D.Coy support in SANDBAG ALLEY	

Army Form C. 2118.

WAR DIARY
or
INTELLIGENCE SUMMARY.
(Erase heading not required.)

JANUARY
7/R KINGS R.S. Part II

Place	Date	Hour	Summary of Events and Information	Remarks and references to Appendices
FRONT LINE	JAN. 3		B.H.Q. still in the lines. Coy very quiet and normal. Men working on enforcement	
			Reliveces and 2 Company moved P.S.	
	9/1/18		Officer JOINING	
	13/1/18		Capt. L.W.P. YATES reported to unit.	
	3/1		MAJOR R.B. KERR M.C. from hospital	
			C/E. J. BAILY reported for duty	
			CASUALTIES	
			Off. Nil	
			O.R. Killed 3	
			Wounded 18	
			Accdtl. 3	
			Missing 2	
			31	
	4/1/18		Officers QUITTING	
	14/1/18		Capt. Cw. Stainforth. R.I.Hosp.	
	27/1/18		2/Lt. K.A.E. LINDOP to Eng. Sick.	
	24/1/18		Lt. G. HINKESLEY to Hosp.	
			Lt. J.R. McILROY M.C.F.Hosp.	

ORyWm
3/-1/18
Wm

Headquarters,
    16th Division.

49th Inf. Bde. No. B.M.C. 13/233 - 17 1 18.

> H.Q.,
> 16TH DIVISION.
> 944
> 17-1-18

Sent

Attached is Report received from 7/8th R. Innis Fus.

There is no doubt that the S.O.S. was sent up, but owing to the Very Lights being fired at the time only the Green Lights were seen and these were taken for enemy Signals.

                                                Captain,
        for Lieut. Col. Comdg. 49th Inf. Brigade.

Headquarters,
49th Inf. Brigade.

At 3.45 this morning, January 17th, the enemy put down a heavy barrage along the East side of HEYTHROP POST. The vicinity of F.4.central was also shelled.

After about 5 minutes, this lifted about 200 yards, and a party of the enemy, about 100 strong attempted to make their way through the wire, some of them getting to our posts at F.4.b.80.40. These were fired upon by Lewis Gun at this point, and also by posts a short distance on either flank. The Lewis Gun on North side of the post was able to bring some fire to bear on enemy. The first mentioned gun was rushed by enemy. No.1 was wounded and the gun and remainder of the team taken prisoner.

Altogether the casualties amount to 1 O.R. killed, 7 O.R. wounded, 7 O.R. missing.

The officer on watch states that very few of the enemy entered the trench, most of the party bombing it from No Man's Land. Smoke bombs were used.

Signal communication by wire was cut off immediately the bombardment was started, and owing to the exceeding bad state of the trenches it took some four hours before repairs were completed.

Just before 4 a.m. two green lights were sent up by the enemy in front of our line, followed by 2 reds and 2 whites, repeated twice. The Corporal with the Officer on watch sent up the S.O.S. twice but owing to confusion of different coloured lights at this time, and owing to the fact that lights sent up by enemy were same colour the artillery did not act upon the S.O.S. signal.

When bombardment commenced retaliation was asked for on QUAIL QUARRY (No. 22), and this was received. After the raid had concluded, No Man's Land was searched for killed or wounded, both ours and enemy, but none was found.

A steel helmet and rifle were found and are sent down herewith.

The raiding party must have come up under cover of dead ground S.E. of LITTLE PRIEL FARM and made their way through our wire under cover of bombardment.

The wire is very thick and deep all along East of HEYTHROP POST and not much knocked about by shell fire.

Had the line been more strongly held, it is improbable that the enemy would have gained a footing in our trench or even approached near enough to bomb it.

Posts are placed in the most advantageous positions, but in spite of this there is no doubt that as long as the line has to be held so thinly, posts are almost certain to be cut off in the event of a strong raiding party coming over.

(sd) A.H.ROBBINS, Captain for
Lieut. Colonel Comdg.
7/8th R. Innis Fus.

17.1.18.

SECRET.

Headquarters,

16th Division.

49th Inf. Bde. No. B.M.C. 13/233/1   17.1.18.

In forwarding attached report the following remarks are submitted :-

(i) I would urge that the S.O.S. Signal be changed. In the confusion of lights that arose it was difficult to pick out the S.O.S.

(ii) There is ground for believing that the N.C.O. who fired the S.O.S. did not elevate his rifle sufficiently.

(iii) The artillery observers report that they saw no coloured lights of any kind.

(iv) The present positions of Posts and the garrison of same are considered sufficient.

(v) Undoubtedly the state of the trench prevented rapid movement, thus to a certain extent favouring the enemy enterprise.

(sd) R.K.C.WELDON Lt.Col.

Commanding 49th Infantry Brigade.

SECRET

Headquarters,
16th Division.

49th Inf. Bde. No. B.M.C. 13/233/1 - 17-1-18.

In forwarding attached report the following remarks are submitted :-

(i) I would urge that the S.O.S. Signal be changed. In the confusion of lights that arose it was difficult to pick out the S.O.S.

(ii) There is ground for believing that the N.C.O. who fired the S.O.S. did not elevate his rifle sufficiently.

(iii) The artillery observers report that they saw no coloured lights of any kind.

(iv) The present positions of Posts and the garrison of same are considered sufficient.

(v) Undoubtedly the state of the trench prevented rapid movement, thus to a certain extent favouring the enemy enterprise.

Lieut. Colonel,
Commanding 49th Infantry Brigade.

Headquarters,

49th Infantry Brigade.

Last night at 3.50 a.m. a heavy barrage was put down on HEYTHROP POST. The enemy about 100 strong came over and gained a footing in our trenches, immediately behind the artillery.

We suffered following casualties :-
- 1 killed.
- 5 wounded.
- 6 missing, presumed Prisoners of War.

The post has been reinforced by one platoon of the Support Company.

The S.O.S? was sent up twice, and no action followed from our artillery.

The above report has been received by Battalion H.Q. at 6.30 a.m., received at 6 a.m. at Advanced Battalion Headquarters from O.C. Left Company.

At 4 p.m. O.C. Right Company rang up H.Q. and said a barrage had been put down on HEYTHROP POST. He thought the S.O.S. had been put up on his left but was not certain.

Retaliation was asked for immediately and received (Bde. Concentration No. 22).

We rang up Advanced Battalion Headquarters, who were safe and did not known what was happening.

Wires to Left Coy. Headquarters (HEYTHROP POST) were cut and no communication was obtained.

The sentries at Battalion Headquarters were questioned by the Adjutant and said that they had seen no S.O.S., but that they had seen 2 single Green Lights and 2 single Red Lights which they took to be enemy lights. This statement was also corroborated by sentries of 49th M.G. Company.

The M.G. Company opened fire in short bursts as they imagined that something was the matter. Their officer was out and the teams standing to at 4.15 a.m.

Bde. was informed at the time the barrage was firing.

Further details will follow as soon as obtained from the front line.

(sd) A.H.Robbins, Capt. for
Lieut. Colonel.
Comdg. 7/8th R. Innis Fus.

17.1.18.

Headquarters,
49th Inf. Brigade.

At 3.45 a.m. this morning, January 17th, the enemy put down a heavy barrage along the East side of HEYTHROP POST. The vicinity of F.4.central was also shelled.

After about 5 minutes, this lifted about 200 yards, and a party of the enemy, about 100 strong, made their way through the wire, some of them getting to our post at F.4.b.80.40. These were fired upon by Lewis Gun at this point, and also by posts a short distance on either flank. The Lewis Gun on North side of the post was able to bring some fire to bear on enemy. The first mentioned gun was rushed by enemy. No. 1 was wounded and the gun and remainder of the team taken prisoner.

Altogether the casualties amount to 1 O.R. killed, 7 O.R. wounded, 7 O.R. missing.

The officer on watch states that very few of the enemy entered the trench, most of the party bombing it from No Man's Land. Smoke smoke bombs were used.

Signal communication by wire was cut off immediately the bombardment was started, and owing to the exceeding bad state of the trenches it took some four hours before repairs were completed.

Just before 4 a.m. two green lights were sent up by the enemy in front of our line, followed by 2 reds and 2 whites, repeated twice. The Cpl with the officer on watch sent up the S.O.S. twice but owing to confusion of different coloured lights at this time, and owing to the fact that lights sent up by enemy were same colour the artillery did not act upon the S.O.S. signal.

When bombardment commenced retaliation was asked for on QUAIL QUARRY (No. 22), and this was received. After the raid had concluded, No Man's Land was searched for killed or wounded, both ours and enemy, but noone was found.

A steel helmet and rifle were found and are sent down herewith.

The raiding party must have come up under cover of dead ground S.E. of LITTLE PRIEL FARM and made their way through our wire under cover of bombardment.

The wire is very thick and deep all along East of HEYTHROP POST and not much knocked about by shell fire.

Had the line been more strongly held, it is improbable that the enemy would have gained a footing in our trench or even approached near enough to bomb it.

Posts are placed in the most advantageous positions, but in spite of this there is no doubt that as long as the line has to be held so thinly, posts are almost certain to be cut off in the event of a strong raiding party coming over.

(sd) A.H.ROBBINS, Captain for
Lieut. Colonel Comdg.
17-1-18.   7/8th R. Innis Fus.

Dispositions 16/1/18
7/8th R Innis Fus

A J Walker Lt Col

WAR DIARY.

FOR MONTH OF FEBRUARY, 1918.

VOLUME:- 6

UNIT:- 4/8th R. Inniskilling Fusrs.

WAR-DIARY or INTELLIGENCE-SUMMARY.

Army Form C. 2118.

FEBRUARY 1/8 R INNIS FUS
Page 5

Place	Date	Hour	Summary of Events and Information	Remarks and references to Appendices
FEB 1st			The Batt. was in Bde Res. Very quiet	JW
FRONT LINE	FEB 3rd		The Batt. was relieved by the 9th R. Dublin Fus. in the Right Subsector, on relief the	JW
Divisional			Batt. moved by train to HAMEL	JW
RESERVE	FEB 5th to FEB 7th		The Bn. spent it days noting cleaning and commenced training, when assembly moved to VILLERS FAUCON on the 7th Feb	JW
	FEB 7		The ARMY Commander visited the area and presented ribbons to officers and men	JW
	FEB 7		The Batt. was moved to VILLERS FAUCON where working parties were provided to dig the CORPS defence line.	JW
Bde RESERVE	FEB 14		The Batt. moved into Bde Reserve in LEFT SECTION of Divisional Bnd. 2Coys A-C. at SAULCOURT, 2Coys and Batt HQ at EPEHY relieving at has places the 1st EAST YORKS REGT. 21st Division	JW
	FEB 14 to FEB 18		Batt. provided working parties ≤ day and improve the defences of the village	JW

WAR DIARY
or
INTELLIGENCE SUMMARY.
(Erase heading not required.)

Army Form C. 2118.
FEBRUARY   7/8 R. INNIS. FUS
PAGE 7

Place	Date	Hour	Summary of Events and Information	Remarks and references to Appendices
			OFFICERS JOINING.	
	FEB. 8.		MAJOR J.S CROTHERS posted to Bat. from 7/R IRISH FUS	
	"	9	Capt. H.G. GROOMBRADGE joined the do do	
	"	12	" C.H. STAINFORTH M.C. " " from staff.	
	"	17	Lt. J.R. McILROY M.C. " "	
				HONORS.
				BELGIAN Croix de Guerre
				3230 Sgt CONWAY A
				24456 " McTAGGART P
			OFFICERS QUITTING.	
	FEB 14		Capt. H.A GREEN M.C. to Eng. (6 mos rest)	
	"	15	Lt. C.M. FRANCIS " do	
	"	16	Capt. C.H STAINFORTH M.C. posted to 1st R. MUNSTER FUS	
	"	19	Lt. C.J. METCALFE to Eng. for brain army	
	"	22	Lt. H.G. GROOM BRADGE to Eng. (6 mo rest)	
	Feb 29		2/Lt E. ILLINGWORTH " " died	
			Casualties: 1.O.R. Wounded	

O.Wakefield Lt.Col
Lieut-Colonel, Commanding
7(S) Battalion R. Innis. Fusiliers.

WAR DIARY
or
INTELLIGENCE SUMMARY.

(Erase heading not required.)

Army Form C. 2118.

FEBRUARY 7/8 R INNIS FUS PAGE 6

Place	Date	Hour	Summary of Events and Information	Remarks and references to Appendices
FRONT LINE	Feb 18.		The Bn. relieved the 2nd Batt. Royal Irish Regt. in RIGHT subsector of LEFT SECTOR. A + C Coys holding front line. A on the right. B Coy on the LEFT. B Coy in SUPPORT. D Coy in RESERVE. Two lines passed very quietly. Fighting and defensive patrols were sent out each night on the front but failed to come in contact with the enemy.	
	Feb 21	4.45am	The S.O.S. signal was fired on the LEFT (they say not) and was repeated by us. The situation LEFT Coy and at Batt. HQ. Artillery Barrage was put down by us. became normal about 5.30 pm	
	Feb 25		B Coy relieved A Coy in RIGHT FRONT. D Coy relieved C Coy in LEFT FRONT on completion A Coy moved to SUPPORT and C Coy to RESERVE	
	Feb 26/28		The Batt. was relieved by 7th (S.I.H) R. IRISH REGT. On completion of relief the Batt. moved into Bgde Support at EPEHY. 2Coys being held in Bgde RESERVE under direct orders of G.O.C. H.Q. Inf. Bgde. The time spent in working parties and improving the defences of the village.	

WAR DIARY
or
INTELLIGENCE SUMMARY.
(Erase heading not required.)

Army Form C. 2118.

FEBRUARY
7/8 R INNIS FUS
Page 7

Place	Date	Hour	Summary of Events and Information	Remarks and references to Appendices
SUPPORT	1918 Feb 28		The Batt: was relieved by the 6th Batt: Leicester Regt, and on completion of relief moved to Corps Reserve at ST EMELIE. Coys in CUTTING CAMP E.23.b.9.2. Bat: H.Q. at E24.a.9.2. The Batt: waiting in readiness to move to defence of ST EMELIE if necessary.	

A.J. Mulcahy, Lt Col
" Lieut.-Colonel, Commanding."
7/8(S) Battalion R. Innis. Fusiliers.

49th Brigade.
16th Division.

7/8th BATTALION

ROYAL INNISKILLING FUSILIERS

MARCH 1918

Army Form C. 2118.

WAR DIARY
INTELLIGENCE SUMMARY.
(Erase heading not required.)

8th R Innis Fus March 1918

Vol E 22

Place	Date	Hour	Summary of Events and Information	Remarks and references to Appendices
ST EMILIE	1st		The Bn moved into the front line trenches. Bn Hd Qrs Bapo Boulogne.	
		1/2 4 am	Enemy raided "a" Coy capturing two prisoners. Raid was preceded by a heavy trench mortar bombardment.	
RONSSOY	8th		The Bn was relieved by the 2nd Royal Irish Regt and moved back to the defences of RONSSOY.	
	12th		Bn relieved South Irish Horse in front line. Bn had Qrs at LANCASTER HOUSE ST EMILIE	
	20th		The Bn was relieved by the 2nd Royal Irish Regiment. It moved back to the defences of RONSSOY.	
	21st		The German attack was launched at dawn in a thick fog. The enemy bombardment was very heavy. Bn Hd Qrs in the centre of RONSSOY, had no knowledge of the attack until the enemy was	

WAR DIARY
or
INTELLIGENCE SUMMARY.
(Erase heading not required.)

Place	Date	Hour	Summary of Events and Information	Remarks and references to Appendices

apart them. They had come in from the Right flank of the Bn. Bn. had on fight their way out suffering heavy casualties Lieut Col Wadling was wounded, the 2nd in command Major Carr DSO MC was captured. The Adjutant Capt A Wilkinson so amazing the signalling officer Lieut HA Wilkinson was killed the intelligence officer Lieut JR McElroy MC was subsequently wounded in the fighting that followed. the company officer came out of the line consequently it is impossible to form a connected narrative of what happened. The remnants of the Battalion fell back and took up a position on the BROWN LINE at ST EMILIE

After some severe fighting the Bn. was ordered to fall back, and the remains of the Bde were formed into the 3rd Prov. Inf. Bde. Bn. under Major Harrison of the 2nd Royal Irish Regt. This Bn.

Army Form C. 2118.

WAR DIARY
or
INTELLIGENCE SUMMARY.
(Erase heading not required.)

3 /8th R. Innis. Fus.   **Two**   **March 18**

Place	Date	Hour	Summary of Events and Information	Remarks and references to Appendices

Raid on 7/8/18 [?]

2. ... back to HAMEL...
repeated attacks...

3. No action with the Enemy dept. on the 22nd March.
...the following officers... Lieut McKeown...
... Capt Leo J. Alley M.C. ...
and Lieut P.J. Nulty who returned from leave on the 22nd March.

4. ... a rear guard action which was subsequently fought at AMIENS...
The Bn came out of the action with the following casualties:—

Casualties —
Off / O.R.

Killed   3 / 13
Died of Wds   1 / 13
Wounded   4 / 200
Prisoners   8 / ...
Missing   2 / 500
Total   18 / 433

F.W. Martin
Captain + Adjt.
for O.C. 8th Bn. Royal Inniskilling Fusrs.

Raid on 7th/8th Inniskillings on
night 4th/5th March.

1. Post raided was at F.18.C.95.80. –
about junction of GLEN LANE with DOD
TRENCH.

   Strength of Post.   1 N.C.O. & 8 O.R.

   Two men on sentry; remainder near by.

2. The night was extremely dark and
misty, with a strong wind blowing. This
made it impossible to hear shouts or calling
even at a short distance. It was also
said to be too bad to use visual.

3. Hostile raiding party is estimated at
30. Of these about 6 actually entered our
trench.

4. Sequence of events was as follows:—

   About 2.30 am. Desultory shelling on right
company began. This lasted some 20 minutes
and then died down.

   3 am. Enemy put down a very heavy barrage.

   3.5 am First S.O.S. signal sent up by
officer on duty. This failed to ignite.
A second attempt was successful. The
message was repeated in front line, at
QUEUCHETTES WOOD and at Bn. HQ.

   3.8 am First guns opened.
   3.20 am Remaining guns opened on telephonic S.O.S.
   3.40 am Situation again normal.

W 151

HQ 49th Inf Bde
(Brigade Major)

Your BMC 13/272 of 5th inst, received 6th inst

Due regard has been paid to orders relating to patrols, but I must again draw your attention to the weather conditions on night 4/5th. The Company Commander considered that if protective patrols were sent out, they would be of no use, owing to a high wind, & sleet blowing towards our lines, making it quite impossible to see or hear to any effect. Again, the men were new to the ground & on such a night it is almost certain that some of them would have been lost. Consequently, it was left to the activity of Lewis Guns & rifle posts to cover the front from 10.30 pm onwards. These facts are upheld by other officers who were in the front line on the night in question.

It is pointed out that all-night patrolling has practically put an end to L.G. & rifle fire at night, for obvious reasons.

2

Regarding the question raised by the Brigade Commander as to why it was not discovered that the SOS grenades were defective: to all outward appearances, they were in perfect condition, & one of those which failed to ignite had only just been taken out of the damp-proof tin canister at Co. HQ. Every precaution is taken with the grenades in order to prevent them from becoming damp.

On two previous occasions I have found that they are defective, & I reported it. Indeed, the first time I saw them, in July last, some were fired for instruction, & one was a "dud".

The remaining men of the post raided, were quite close, — 10 or 15 yards away, & 3 of them did fire at the enemy, & warning was also passed along to next post northwards that the enemy had got into our trench.

They might have put up a much better fight were it not for the fact that the Corporal in charge made off to warn the Company Comm.dr

3

when he saw we were raided. He is consequently under close arrest & summary of evidence is being taken.

@JWalker Lt Col
Commdg 7/8th R Inniskg us.

7/3/18

HQ 49th Inf Bde.
(Brigade Major)

About 2.30 am this morning, the enemy commenced desultary shelling of the southern portion of battalion front; this lasted some 20 minutes & then died off. At 3 am enemy put down a very heavy barrage, the principal points affected being as follows

DUNCAN AV; from front line to about F.18.a.70.30; about 20 direct hits with Minenwerfer

Point of GUILLEMONT SALIENT, Minenwerfer

F.17.d (central)   5.9's
F.23.b.8.8   4.2s & 77mm.
Front line generally   Ditto.

At 3.5 am, the officer on watch on left company front, sent up S.O.S grenade, but it failed to ignite,- however, another was sent up, & repeated on front line, QUEUCHETTE'S WOOD, & Bn. HQ.

Guns were very late in opening fire, which did not commence until 3.20 am

Shortly after O.C Left Coy reported

2

3 men missing, but one was
afterwards found.
 Apparently a party of the enemy
about 30 strong approached our
line at F 18 c 95.80, & some of
them (about 6, judging by the
marks made where they entered)
entered the trench, made for a
post some 50 yards up the trench
& took the two sentries prisoners,
leaving a few stick bombs behind
them.
 By 3.40 am, situation was again
normal.
 Communication was kept all the
time by wire with Left Front Coy,
but Right Front & Support were cut
off for some time, & runners
had to be used. The night was
too misty to use visual.
 Casualties, 2 OR killed
             2 OR missing.
Vickers Guns had commenced
slow rate of fire before heavy
bombardment commenced, &
consequently answered S.O.S.
immediately.

Regarding the post which was
raided, its strength was 1 NCO
& 8 OR, two men being on sentry.
The remainder were near by, but
did not discover what was happening
until too late. It was extremely
dark & misty, & a strong wind
was blowing, making it impossible
to hear shouts or calling even
at a very short distance.

Altogether, 4 of the SOS grenades
used failed to ignite.

Information given herewith
has already been given to Div.
Intelligence Officer & Asst. Bde-Major.

A.J. Walkey Lt Col
Commdg 7/8th R. Innis. Fus.

5/3/18

Army Form C. 2118.

WAR DIARY
INTELLIGENCE SUMMARY.
(Erase heading not required.)

1/8th Royal Innis. Fus. April 18. Vol 27

Place	Date	Hour	Summary of Events and Information	Remarks and references to Appendices
	April 4th		The Battalion was relieved and moved into rest billets	
E.V.	10th		Major R.J. Kerr M.C. took over command of the Battalion we had only	
	11th		Bn arrived at REMILLY from SOMME AREA	
	15.		A composite Bn called the 149th Inf. Bde Composite Bn was formed under command of Major R.J. Kerr m.c.	
			This Bn consisted of the 1/8th Royal Innis Fus, 2nd Royal Irish Regt and 1st (0.3.H) Royal Innis. Regt.	
	14.		The Composite Bn moved to STEENBECQUE to dig G.H.Q. line	
	23		All ranks of the 1/8th Royal Innis Fus less a training staff of 3 Officers and 43 O.Ranks and transport were transferred to the 2nd Royal Irish Regiment	
	26th		The training staff proceeded to back area of train as cadre of Awaiting Armies Bn. D	2 Ind

Army Form C. 2118.

WAR DIARY
or
INTELLIGENCE SUMMARY.
(Erase heading not required.)

Instructions regarding War Diaries and Intelligence Summaries are contained in F. S. Regs., Part II. and the Staff Manual respectively. Title pages will be prepared in manuscript.

April 1918.

Place	Date	Hour	Summary of Events and Information	Remarks and references to Appendices
	April			
	30th		The Nursing Staff moved off again to the STEEN BECQUE AREA and received 860 Units Reinforcements and commenced work in G.H. Ahn. Recognition of Bt. 1/6th Royal Inns. Fusiliers (Rev. Roy.)	
STEEN BECQUE			Honors	
			Military Medal 36444 Ae W. McHugh	
			Bar to Military Cross Lieut J. R. McElroy M.C.	
			H.W. Monk Captain & Adj. for OC 1/6th Royal Inns. Killing Fusiliers	

Army Form C. 2118.

WAR DIARY
or
INTELLIGENCE SUMMARY.

(Erase heading not required.)

Instructions regarding War Diaries and Intelligence Summaries are contained in F.S. Regs., Part II. and the Staff Manual respectively. Title pages will be prepared in manuscript.

/5th/ Royal Sussex Regt.   Month and year: May 1918   Vol 26

Place	Date	Hour	Summary of Events and Information	Remarks and references to Appendices
STEENBECQUE	1st		Bat. Transport Staff consisting of 6 officers + NCOs + Men met	
			Capt FW Martin MC, Lt JA Mortin MC, Capt A Leland, Capt J Nally	
			Capt Whitell, Rev. F.W. and Lt O'Kanks	
	16		Bat. moved to LEDINGHEM	
	18		Bat. moved to SANER at base transport base than had ½ on route	
			part transferred to to 4th American Div.	
	19		Bat. moved to ERENCQ	
	31		Battalion still at PRENCQ	
			Officers Joining	
			Capt F.W. Norton MC Reported for duty	
			Capt. G.J. Healy MC R.B.J Reported for duty 10.5.18	Major W. Lee MC Lydd ... Jan 28.5.18
			Capt M. Farhid R.bol R.S... Reported for duty 26.5.18	
			Capt L.W. Singh Middlesex Regt. Reported for duty 30.5.18	

F.W. Martin Capt & Adjt
for OC 5th the Royal Sussex Regt

SECRET

Cover for Documents.

Nature of Enclosures.

49th. Infantry Brigade.

ADMINISTRATIVE INSTRUCTIONS

Notes, or Letters written.

Copy of No. 2 Annexed to F.O. 24.7.17

S E C R E T.   Copy No.....

49th INFANTRY BRIGADE.
SPECIAL ADMINISTRATIVE INSTRUCTIONS.

I N D E X

1. Introductory.
2. Pack Transport.
3. Accommodation.
3A. Accommodation - Wagon and Transport Lines (Contd).
4. Burial Orders.
5. Salvage.
6. Water Supply.
6A. Water Supply - Back Areas.
6B. Forward Water Supply.
7. Medical Arrangements.
8. Straggler Posts.
9. Reinforcement Depot.
10. Prisoners of War.
11. Ordnance Services.
12. March Discipline.
13. Veterinary Arrangements.
14.
15.
16.
17.
18.
19.
20.

SECRET.  Copy No. 5

49th INFANTRY BRIGADE.

SPECIAL ADMINISTRATIVE INSTRUCTIONS No. 1.

Reference Maps Sheet 27 N.E. and 28 N.W. 1/20.000

3.7.17.

INTRODUCTORY.

1. Special Administrative Instructions as regards forthcoming operations will be issued from time to time. So far as is possible, a separate subject will be dealt with in each Instruction.

2. These Instructions will be issued under some or all of the following headings, but not necessarily in the same order:-

Introductory - Accommodation - Supplies - Water for men - Water for animals - Medical Arrangements - Ammunition - Police Arrangements for Stragglers Posts - Light Railways - Tramways - Roads - Traffic Control - March Discipline - Transport Lines - Organization of Pack Transport - Surplus Kits - Corps Reinforcement Camp - R.E. Stores - Ordnance Stores/

2.

Ordnance Stores - Railheads - Collection and escort
of Prisoners - Salvage - Burials.

3. The opening paragraphs of each Instruction will
deal with the arrangements up to and including
ZERO. The concluding paragraphs will give a
forecast of the Administrative Arrangements proposed for the period following ZERO.

4. Amendments to these Instructions will have to
be issued from time to time, but, so far as is
possible, when many amendments become necessary,
the Instruction affected will be cancelled and
a new one issued.

5. Units will push forward their Administrative
arrangements, in anticipation of the issue of these
instructions, on the lines laid down in S.S. 135,
"Instructions for the Training of Divisions for
Offensive Action".

6. All Brigade Special Administrative Instructions
will be issued to the undermentioned:-

```
        G.C.C..........  Copy No. 1.
        Brigade Major.    "    "  2.
2/R. Irish Regt.....     "    "  3.
7/R. Innis. Fus.....     "    "  4.
8/R. Innis. Fus.....     "    "  5.
7/8th R. Irish Fus..     "    "  6.
49th M.G.Coy........     "    "  7.
49th T.M. Battery...     "    "  8.
Asst. Staff Captain.     "    "  9.
16th Div. Q.........     "    "  10 & 11
War Diary ..........     "    "  12 & 13
File................     "    "  14.
```

3.

Para 6 Contd.

Only so far as they concern them will Instructions

be sent to O.C. Field Coy. R.E., O.C. Train Coy.,

and O.C. Field Ambulance.

H P Bowen
Captain,
Staff Captain,
49th Infantry Brigade.

Copy No. 1. G.O.C.
2. Brigade Major.
3. 2/R. Irish Regt.
4. 2/R. Innis. Fus.
5. 8/R. Innis. Fus.
6. 7/8th R. Irish Fus.
7. 49th M.G. Coy.
8. 49th T.M. Battery.
9. Asst. Staff Captain.
10)
11) 16th Div. Q.
12)
13) War Diary.
14 File.

SECRET.   Copy No. 12

8th. R. INNISKILLING FUSILIERS OPERATION ORDER No.111 - 7/7/17.

Reference { 1/20,000 Sheet 27 A.S.E.
          { 1/40,000 Sheet 27
          { 1/100,000 HAZEBROUCK 5A.

1. The 49th. Inf. Bde. will march to the RUBROUCK AREA on July 8th.

2. Order of March - 7th. R. Innis. Fus., 2nd. R. Irish Regt., 7/8th. R. Irish Fus., 8th. R. Innis. Fus., 49th. M.G.C., 49th. T.M.B., 49th. I.B., H.Q., 144th. Coy. A.S.C.

3. The Starting Point for the Battn. will be the road junction W.4.d.4.2. The Battn. will be formed up along the LEULINE - ETREHEM Road with the head of the Battn. at Cross Roads W.4.d.2.1. in the order H.Q., C, A, D, B, Coys. ready to move off by 6.10 a.m.

4. Route. TATINGHEM - St. MARTIN-AU-LAERT - ST. OMER - BROXEELE to destination "O". Area H.7.13., G.12.18.

5. 2/Lieut. R.E. Palmgren will proceed at sufficient distance in front of the Battn. to give warning to Traffic Control.

6. Battn. Transport, including Baggage Wagons, will accompany Battn.

7. Two motor lorries, one of which is to be shared with 7/8th. R. Irish Fus. will be available for conveyance of men's packs only, and will report to Battn. H.Q. about 7 a.m. Each Coy. will leave behind one man to act as loading party.

8. Usual halts will be observed.

9. Dress. Skeleton marching order, haversack carried on the back, steel helmets will be worn. All mess tins, mugs, &c., to be carried inside haversack.
Only brakesmen will march behind vehicles. Lewis Guns and magazines will be carried on limbers.

10. Brigade H.Q., will close at TATINGHEM at 6.35 a.m. and will open at RUBROUCK on arrival.

11. O.C. "C" Coy. will detail one platoon to stay behind and make sure that the billets of Battn. are left scrupulously clean. He will render a certificate to Orderly Room to this effect on arrival at destination. Transport Officer will make his own arrangements.

12. ROUTINE. Reveille 3.30 a.m. Breakfast 4.15 a.m. Officers' valises to be outside billets at 4.30 a.m. Mess Cart and Maltese Cart packed by 5.30 a.m.

13. ACKNOWLEDGE.

                                                R. Loggins
                                                    Lieut.,
                                                 a/Adjutant.
Issued through Signals :   8th. R. Inniskilling Fusrs.

Copy No. 1 to O.C. "A" Coy.
  "   "   2 .. .. "B" "
  "   "   3 .. .. "C" "
  "   "   4 .. .. "D" "
  "   "   5 .. Capt. H.A. Green M.C.
  "   "   6 .. Medical Officer.
  "   "   7 .. Quartermaster.
  "   "   8 .. Transport Officer.
  "   "   9 .. 2/Lieut. R.E. Palmgren
  "   " 10 .. R. S. M.
  "   " 11 .. H.Q., 49th. I.B.
  "   " 12/13 Retained.

SECRET.   Copy No. 12

8th R. INNISKILLING FUSILIERS OPERATION ORDER NO. 112. 8/7/17.

Reference, 1/40,000 Sheet 27.

1. The 49th I.B., will march to the WINNIZEELE Area tomorrow July 9th.

2. Order of March - 7th R. Innis. Fus. 7/8th R. Irish Fus. 8th R. Innis. Fus. 2nd R. Irish Regt., 49th M.G.C. 49th T.M.B. 49th I.B. H.Q. 1 4th Coy. A.S.C. 113th F.A.

3. The Starting Point for the Battalion will be Road Junction H.2.d.2.8. The Battn. will be formed up along road running S.W. of this point in the order H.Q. "D" "B" "A" "C" Coys. ready to move off by 5.10 a.m.

4. Route.- WORMHOUDT - Road Junction C.17.a.5.8.- KIEKEN PUT - LOOGEHOEK.

5. 2/Lieut. J.L. Charlesworth will proceed at sufficient distance in front of the Battn. to give warning to Traffic Control.

6. Intervals of 500 yards will be kept between Battalions.

7. Usual halts will be observed.

8. Battalion Transport, including Baggage Wagons, will accompany Battn.

9. Two motor Lorries, one of which is to be shared with 7/8th R. Irish Fus. will be available for carrying mens' packs only.
   Each Coy. and H.Q. will detail one man _only_ to act as loading party.

10. Dress - Skeleton Marching Order, haversack carried on the back; steel helmets will be worn. All Mess tins, mugs, etc., to be carried inside haversack.
    Only brakesmen will march behind vehicles. Lewis Guns and Magazines will be carried on Limbers.

11. Brigade H.Q. will close at RUBROUCK at 6 a.m. and will open at WINNIZEELE on arrival.

12. O.C. "D" Coy., will detail one platoon to stay behind and make sure that the Billets of Battn., are left scrupulously clean. He will render a certificate to Orderly Room to that effect on arrival at Destination. Transport Officer will make his own arrangements.

13. ROUTINE. Reveille, 2.30 a.m. Breakfasts 3.15 a.m.
    Officers' valises to be outside billets at 4 a.m.
    Mess Cart and Maltese Cart packed by 4.30 a.m.

14. ACKNOWLEDGE.

Issued through Signals at 7.50 p.m.

Copy. No. 1 to O.C. "A" Coy.
"   "   2 " "   "B" "
"   "   3 " "   "C" "
"   "   4 " "   "D" "
"   "   5 " Capt. H.A. Green, M.C.
"   "   6 " Medical Officer.
"   "   7 " Quartermaster.
"   "   8 " Transport Officer.
"   "   9 " 2/Lieut. J.L. Charlesworth.
"   "   10 " R.S.M.
"   "   11 " H.Q. 49th I.B.
"   "   12/13 Retained.

                                                    Lieut.
                                                    A/Adjutant.
                                      8th R. Inniskilling Fusiliers......

SECRET.   Copy No. 5

49th INFANTRY BRIGADE.

SPECIAL ADMINISTRATIVE INSTRUCTION No. 4.

BURIAL ORDERS.

1. A Divisional Burial Section will be maintained ready to take up work when heavy fighting takes place; strength as under:-

    Officer............. 1.
    N.C.O's............. 2.
    Men................ 20.
    Batman............... 1.

    The above will be detailed by O.C. 11th Hampshire Regt. (Pioneers).
    This Section will be augmented as necessary by men of Corps Labour Companies, or otherwise.

2. The following Chaplains will be attached to the Burial Section during heavy fighting, and will be detailed by name by the senior Chaplains concerned when ordered:-

    C. of E. Chaplain........ 1.
    Roman Catholic........... 1.
    Presbyterian or
    Non-conformist Chaplain..1. }

3. The Divisional Burial Section is intended to assist Units in the burial of their dead in the event of heavy casualties or of an advance, and to ensure that no bodies in the Divisional Area are left unburied any longer than is absolutely necessary.

    In order to avoid unnecessary casualties the Division will define from time to time a line behind which Divisional Burial Sections will operate, and will indicate to the Divisional Burial Officer the place where casualties have occurred.

    The Divisional Burial Officer will at the same time keep in close touch with the Headquarters of Brigades that are in action, so as to obtain early information as to where his assistance is required.

4. He will get in touch with the Corps Burial Officer who will allot him a detachment of a Labour Company (probably 100 men) with whom he will co-operate in the event of heavy fighting.

5. He will see that the personal effects of men are placed in the small bags provided, labelled; and placed together in sand-bags by units, Brigades etc., and forwarded to Corps Burial Officer.

                                        Contd. Page 2./

2.

6. He will complete registration forms for all men buried and forward them to the Corps Burial Officer who will be responsible for sending on the copies to:-

    D.A.G., G.H.Q. 3rd Echelon.
    D.G.R. and E. War Office.
    ~~Corps G.R.U. Officer.~~ O.C Graves Registration unit of Army
    XIX Corps "A".

Necessary extracts will be forwarded by the Divisinal Burial Officer direct to units to which buried men belong.

7. The Divisional Burial Officer will make out Registration Forms from information sent by units as to burials carried our regimentally and will forward them to the Corps Burial Officer together with personal effects which he will sort out and place in bags before despatch.

Brigades and units will ensure that this procedure is carried out, as it is only by their careful co-operation with the Burial Officer that this system can work satisfactorily.

8. The Divisional Burial Officer will receive all returns and personal effects of buried men, and will keep his Divisional Headquarters informed of his position, so that all units can be informed.

9. The Corps Burial Officer is empowered to call upon Divl. Burial Sections to assist other sections outside the Divl. Area, should such a course appear to him to be necessary.

10. A 'pro-forma' Burial Return is attached.

                                        2/Lt.
                               A/Staff Captain,
                             49th Infantry Brigade.

15.7.17.

BURIAL RETURN 16th. DIVISION.

(PRO-FORMA).

No. No.	Rank.	Name & Initials.	Bn. & Regt.	Exact place of burial.	By whom buried.	Identification No.

To be pasted in A.B. 152.

INSTRUCTIONS.

1. Remove nothing from dead until placed in grave.
2. Bury, British, French, and German dead separately.
3. Mark flanks of graves with posts if available wire.
4. Enter map reference and nearest land mark in note book.
5. Select unexposed position.
6. Bury Officers with men.
7. Enter particulars as body placed in the grave.
8. Tie up all personal belongings with identity cord, place in bag, write particulars on label.

    (a) Place British in Brigade Sand-bag.
    (b) Place French in Divisional bag marked "Q".
    (c) Place German in Divisional Bag marked "G".

9. Mark all graves with cross and write Serial No. in Book.

S E C R E T. Copy No. 2

49th INFANTRY BRIGADE.

SPECIAL ADMINISTRATIVE INSTRUCTIONS No. 5.

SALVAGE.

1. The 16th Divisional Salvage Company will consist of:-
H.Q. SECTION.

	Offrs.	N.C.O.	R & F.	Total	Remarks.
Sergeants	-	1	-	1	P.B. Men
Corporals.	-	-	2	2	lent to
Privates	-	-	15	15	Div. by Corps.
HEADQUARTERS.					Found from
Commanding Off.	1	-	-	1	Divl. Employ-
Sergeants.	-	1	-	1	ment
Cyclists	-	-	2	2	Coy.
Batman	-	-	1	1	
BRIGADE SECTIONS.					
Corporals.	-	1	-	1	In each
Privates.	-	-	20	20	Inf. Bde.

2. Each Brigade Section will include a proportion of trained bombers who alone will be allowed to handle bombs, grenades and S.A.A., until the latter are pronounced safe.

3. The Salvage Companies of Divisions will be responsible for the Salvage of all derelict arms, ammunition, supplies, and equipment within their Area from YPRES inclusive forward.
   When Divisions are withdrawn, their Salvage Companies will remain and come under direct orders of the Corps Salvage Officer, who will allot each of them definate Areas in which to work.

4. Divisional Salvage Dumps will be formed at suitable sites near road and light railway. Locations of these Dumps will be wired to the Corps Salvage Officer whose Headquarters and Dumps will be at the Railhead. Brigades & Units will form dumps at suitable sites and notify position of same to the next higher formation.

5. The Division is responsible for the transport of all salved material from Brigade or unit Dumps to the Main Divisional Dump. O.C., 16th Divisional Train will detail 2 G.S. Wagons for permanent duty with Divisional Salvage Company on receipt of instructions to do so.

6. Divisional Salvage Officer will wear the Divisional Arm-band with "SALVAGE" in black letters.

16.7.17.

H.F. Leufort.
2/Lt.
A/Staff Captain,
49th Infantry Brigade.

SECRET   Copy No. 5

49th INFANTRY BRIGADE.

SPECIAL ADMINISTRATIVE INSTRUCTION NO. 7.

MEDICAL ARRANGEMENTS.

1. The following Medical Posts will be established:-
Regimental Aid Posts.

Left Division.	Right Division.
Two in OXFORD ROAD.	Two behind CAMBRIDGE ROAD.

Collecting Stations.

Left Division.	Right Division.
St. JEAN.	MENIN ROAD. (I.9.d.4.6.)
POTIJZE Chateau	POTIJZE Chateau.

Advanced Dressing Stations.

Left Division.	Right Division.
Canal Bank. (I.1.b.8.6).	KRUISSTRAAT (H.24.a.5.9)
Prison, YPRES.	Prison, YPRES.

Main Dressing Stations.

Left Division.	Right Division.
RED FARM (G.5.d.8.7)	BRANDHOEK (G.12.b.8.6).

Corps Walking Wounded Collecting Station.
VLAMERTINGHE MILL (H.8.a.9.8).

2. Regimental bearers supplemented by R.A.M.C. Bearers will clear to Regimental Aid Posts.
R.A.M.C. Bearers will clear from Regimental Aid Posts to Collecting Posts.
From Collecting Posts clearing will be by road, and rail. If clearing is by rail, it will be from ST. JEAN to siding at Main Dressing Station.

3. The A.D.S. in the cellars of the YPRES Prison will be shared by both Divisions. In addition to receiving all local wounded from YPRES, in the event of evacuation being held up for any reason, serious wounded cases will be accommodated in this place.

4. Walking wounded will be guided by directing signs skirting the North and South sides of YPRES to the Corps Walking Wounded Collecting Station, whence busses will take them to the C.C.S. Should the roads be free from shelling, lorries will be advanced to H.12.c. see attached sheet (=).

5. As the advance takes place, new collecting posts will be selected, possibly at FREZENBERG and BRIDGE HOUSE, and evacuation will take place from these posts. As the length of the carry will be very considerably increased, additional bearers will be required. These will be obtained either from Field Ambulances of Reserve Divisions, or from Infantry, under Divisional arrangements.

16.7.17.

H.C.Shinfoot.
A/Staff Captain, 49th Inf. Brigade

SECRET.   Copy No. 5

49th INFANTRY BRIGADE.

SPECIAL ADMINISTRATIVE INSTRUCTIONS No. 3.

ACCOMMODATION.

Reference Map Attached.

1. For the purpose of Operations the XIXth Corps Area will be organised as follows (see attached map).

    YPRES   North Area.
    YPRES   South Area.
    BRANDHOEK Area. (Staging Area for reliefs).
    WATOU Area.
    WATOU Artillery Area.
    WINNEZEELE Artillery Area.
    WINNEZEELE Area.

2. On "Z" Day units will be disposed as follows:-

    YPRES North Area   1 Division.
    YPRES South Area   1 Division.
    BRANDHOEK Area   1 Division.
    WATOU Area   1 Division.

    WATOU and WINNEZEELE Artillery Areas will be used for Artillery only as far as possible.

3. In many cases it may be necessary to take sites on growing crops, but where there is a choice of land the owner should be consulted as to what he can spare best.

4. As far as possible, as Units arrive, they will be sent to their permanent sites.

5. Tentage or shelters will be provided for camps, but this is not to be erected till units arrive. The principle has been accepted that NISSEN Huts are allowed for Offices of Division, Brigade, and Battalion etc., Headquarters. When sites have been selected the necessary huts will be demanded from Corps "Q" and erected. These will be used by Divisions now in the Area and handed over to incoming units.

6. Sites for camps will be selected on the principle that regular lines are to be avoided. Advantage is to be taken of all cover to hide the camps.

                                            2/Lt.
                                      A/Staff Captain.
                                     49th Infantry Brigade.

15.7.17.

S E C R E T.   Copy No. 15

8th. ROYAL INNISKILLING FUSILIERS OPERATION ORDER No. 113. - 24/7/17

Ref. Map 1/40.000.
Sheet 27.

1. The 49th. I. B. Group, less 113th. F.A., will march to WATOU No. 2 Area on 26th. July.

2. Order of March - 144th. Coy. A.S.C., 7/8th. R. Irish Fus., 7th. R. Innis. Fus., 2nd. The R. Irish Regt., 8th. R. Innis. Fus., 157th. Fd. Coy. R.E., 49th. M.G. Coy., 49th. T.M.B., H.Q. 49th. I.B.

3. The Battalion, less "B" Coy., will form up on road outside Camp facing North East in order H.Q., A., C., D., Coys., and will be ready to march off at 6.40 a.m. "B" Coy. will join in rear of Battn. at Coy. Billet.

4. The Battalion will pass starting point J.12.b.8.7. at 7.10 a.m. - Route from Starting Point : WATOU - Cross Roads in K.12.c. to L.13.c.4.4.

5. Intervals of 500 yards will be kept between Battalions.

6. Battalion Transport will accompany Battn., moving complete with Baggage Wagons.

7. Dress - Full Marching Order, Steel Helmets will be worn. Lewis Guns and magazines will be carried in limbers.

8. Advance Party : Lieut. C.J. Coggins and 1 N.C.O. and man per Coy. and H.Q. Unit will move off at 2 p.m. on 25th. inst. to take over billets &c., Half Limbered wagon for kits will accompany this party.

9. O. C. "A" Coy will detail one platoon to clean up Camp and billets after the Battalion has marched out. He will render a certificate on arrival at new H.Q. that Camp and Billets were left in a thoroughly clean condition.

10. Routine for 26th. inst. will be as under :-
Reveille 4.15 a.m.   Breakfasts 5 a.m.
Officers' Valises will be stacked outside billets by 5.15 a.m. Valises must be packed tightly and rolled as neatly as possible.
Mess Cart and Maltese Cart to be packed by 6 a.m.

11. Capt. W.R. Maguire will be mounted and will ride ahead of the column at sufficient distance to warn traffic control of approach of Bn.

12. Bde. H.Q. will close at WINNEZEELE at 6.30 a.m. on 26th. inst. and will open at L.13.d.3.4. on arrival.

13. ACKNOWLEDGE.

                                                        Captain.,
                                    Adjutant, 8th. R. Inniskilling Fus.

Issued through Signals at
Copy No. 1 to O.C. "A" Coy.
  "   " 2 "   "   "B" "
  "   " 3 "   "   "C" "
  "   " 4 "   "   "D" "
  "   " 5 " Signalling Officer.
  "   " 6 " 2/Lt. K.H. Borcherds.
  "   " 7 " Lieut. C.J. Coggins.
  "   " 8 " Capt. W.R. Maguire.
  "   " 9 " Quartermaster.
  "   " 10 " Transport Officer.
  "   " 11 " R. S. M.
  "   " 12 " Medical Officer.
  "   " 13 " H.Q. 49th. I. B.
  "   " 14/15 Retained.

SECRET.   Copy No........ 3

8th. ROYAL INNISKILLING FUSILIERS OPERATION ORDER No. 114 - 27-7-17.

Ref. Maps
   1/40.000 Sheet 27
   1/20.000 Sheet 28 N.W.

1. With reference to forthcoming Offensive Operations the 49th. Infantry Brigade will move to BRANDHOEK No. 1 Area on night Y/Z. The date of W Day will be notified later to all concerned.

2. On completion of this move disposition of the Brigade will be as under:

   49th. I.B. H.Q.   RED ROSE CAMP   H.2.c.2.7.
   8th. R. Innis. Fus.   do.   H.1.b.8.0.
   2nd. R. Irish Reg.   DERBY CAMP   H.1.a.8.0.
   7th. R. Innis. Fus.   "B" CAMP   G.6.d.4.4.
   49th. T.M.B.   do. do.   do.
   49th. M.G. Coy.   BEDOUIN CAMP.   G.6.b.2.0.
   7/8th. R. Irish Fus.   QUERY CAMP.   G.6.a.8.2.
   157th. Fd. Coy. R.E.   do.   G.11.d.2.8.
   144th. Coy. A.S.C.   do.   G.15.a.5.2.

3. Units of Brigade move in order named in para. 2.

4. The Battalion will form up facing South on road running from Cross Roads L.1.c.9.0. to L.14.c.3.3. Head of Column at L.14.c.3.3. in order H.Q., A, B, D, C, Coys., Transport, and will be ready to move by 9.50 p.m.
Head of Battalion will pass Starting Point road junction L.9.c.1.9. at 10.20 p.m.

5. Route - L.11.b.8.8. - L.6.c.9.4. - GRAND PLACE POPERINGHE - Main YPRES ROAD.

6. Distances of 500 yards will be maintained between Battalions as far as L.6.c.5.0. East of that point distances of 200 yards will be maintained between Coys. and between rear Coy. and Transport.

7. Capt. W.R. Maguire will be mounted and will precede the Battalion at sufficient distance to warn traffic control of approach. Lamps will be carried at front and rear of Battalion.

8. Advance Party - Quartermaster, 1 N.C.O. and man per Coy., and H.Q., will proceed to RED ROSE CAMP on the morning of "Y" Day moving off from Battalion H.Q. at 9.30 a.m.

9. Billets must be thoroughly clean before moving out. O.C. Coys. and Units will render a certificate to this effect before Battalion moves off.

10. From W. day onwards every precaution is to be taken to conceal the concentration of troops from observation by hostile aircraft.
All movement in the vicinity of huts, camps, or bivouacks is to be restricted to a minimum.
Aeroplane sentries are to be posted by all Coys. and Units.

11. Infantry is to be given precedence of all traffic on X/Y and Y/Z nights, and on Z Day from Zero to Zero plus 3 hours.
Routes allotted and restrictions as to use are to be strictly adhered to.

12. Brigade H.Q. will close at L.13 Central at 10 p.m. on Y/Z Night,
   a. will open at RED ROSE CAMP H.2.c.2.7. on arrival.

13. ACKNOWLEDGE.

                                              W.E.H. Rms
                                                    Captain.,
                          Adjutant, 8th. R. Inniskilling Fusrs.

Issued through Signals at

```
Copy No.  1 to O.C.    "A" Coy.
 ..  ..   2 ..  ..     "B"  "
 ..  ..   3 ..  ..     "C"  "
 ..  ..   4 ..  ..     "D"  "
 ..  ..   5 .. Signal Officer.
 ..  ..   6 .. 2/Lieut. K.H. Borcherds.
 ..  ..   7 .. Quartermaster.
 ..  ..   8 .. Transport Officer.
 ..  ..   9 .. H.Q., 49th. Inf. Bde.
 ..  ..  10 .. Capt. W.R. Maguire.
 ..  ..  11 .. R.  S.  M.
 ..  ..  12/13 Retained.
```

SECRET.

O.C. "A" Coy.
 .. "B" "
 .. "C" "
 .. "D" "
Signalling Officer.
2/Lieut. K.H. Borchards.
Lieut. C.J. Coggins.
2/Lieut. R.V. Polley.
Medical Officer.
Quartermaster.
Transport Officer.

8th. R. Innis. Fus. O.O. 114/1 - 29/7/17.
---

1. In continuation of Operation Order No. 114 dated 27-7-17
...... day was 28th. July.

2. **Advance Parties** Lieut. C.J. Coggins, 1 N.C.O. and man per Coy. and H.Q. will proceed to RED ROSE CAMP to take over, to-morrow 30th. inst. This party will leave present H.Q. at 8.30 a.m.
Os.C. B & D Coys. will each detail 10 bombers who will parade at 6.45 a.m. to-morrow 30th. inst. under 2/Lieut. R.V. Polley and will march to RED ROSE CAMP H.1.b.8.0. 2/Lieut. Polley and 8 O.R. will report to Capt. T.H. Stitt M.C. at Brigade H.Q. (BRANDHOEK No. 1 Area) H.2.c.2.7. at 11.45 a.m. to take over :-

           Mills No. 5 1888
           "P" Bombs   80
           Flares   400
           Very Lights 1"   600
            "   "   1½"   104
           S.O.S. Rockets   30

Lorry containing above will be guided to Camp, where bombs &c., will be detonated and stacked ready for issue.

All above parties will wear full marching order and will carry unexpended portion of day's rations.
Rations for consumption of 1st. August will be delivered at RED ROSE CAMP about 12 Noon to-morrow and will be taken over by Lieut. C.J. Coggins.
The above parties will join the Battalion on its arrival at RED ROSE CAMP.

3. Bombs will be stacked at each Coy. billet ready for issue as under :-
   Per Coy. : Mills No. 5 250
               Mills No. 23 250
               "P" Bombs   18
               Flares   100
               Very Lights 1" ... ... ½ Box.
                "   "   1½" ... ...   20 rounds
               S.O.S. Signal Rifle Grenades 6
   Battn. H.Q. "P" Bombs   8
               Very Lights 1" ... ... 2 Boxes.
                "   "   1½" ... ...   24 rounds
               S.O.S. Signal Rifle Grenades 6

4. Officers' Kits will be stacked outside billets ready for loading by 7.30 p.m. Mess Kits to be ready for loading by 8 p.m. Maltese Cart to be loaded by 8 p.m.

5. Lewis Gun Limbered Wagons will be sent to their Coys. at 3 p.m. for loading.

6. ACKNOWLEDGE

W.E.H. Mun
Captain,,
Adjutant, 8th. R. Inniskilling Fusrs.

SECRET.   Copy No......9...

8th. R. Innis. Fus. S/539 - 30-7-17.

ADMINISTRATIVE INSTRUCTIONS.

The follwoing extracts from 49th. Infantry Brigade Special Administrative Instructions are published for the information and guidance of all Officers :

(1) **BURIAL ARRANGEMENTS.** During heavy fighting a Divisional Burial Section will be maintained - Strength 1 Officer and about 23 Other Ranks. This Section will be reinforced by personnel detailed by Corps Labour Troops. This section is intended to assist Infantry Units in the burial of their dead in the event of heavy casualties, and it will work behind a line defined by D.H.Q. from time to time.

All Officers who are in charge of burial parties should note the following instructions :-
(1) Remove nothing from dead until placed in grave.
(2) Bury British, French and German Dead separately.
(3) Mark flanks of graves with posts - if available wire.
(4) Enter map references and nearest land mark in note book.
(5) Select unexposed position.
(6) Bury Officers with men.
(7) Enter particulars as body placed in grave.
(8) Tie up personal belongings with identity cord; place in bag, write particulars on label.
   Separate sandbags to be kept for each nationality.
(9) Mark graves with cross, and serial number.

Return of men buried in all cases to be rendered to Battn. H.Q. giving the following information :-
(a) No. Rank. Name and initials.   (c) By Whom buried.
(b) Bn., Regt., and exact place of burial. (d) Identification number.

(2) **PRISONERS OF WAR.**
(a) The Right Divisional Cage will be at ECOLE I.9.c.5.2.
(b) The representative of the A.P.M. will give a receipt on A.F.W. 3443 to fighting troops for all prisoners taken over.
(c) Fighting troops who capture prisoners are immediately to search all Officers, and take away from them all documents which are then placed in an empty sandbags and sent with escort to the Divisional Cage. Special attention should be paid to pockets in back skirt of tunics and back of trousers. Personnal belongings and decorations should not be removed.
(d) Rifles of escorts should be loaded and any prisoners attempting to escape should be shot. Escorts must on no account scatter in pursuit.

(3) **MEDICAL ARRANGEMENTS.** Right Division.
Regtl. Aid Posts - Two behind CAMBRIDGE ROAD.
Collecting Stations - MENIN Road I.9.d.4.6.
                     POTIJZE CHATEAU
Advanced Dressing Stations - KRUISSTRAAT (H.24.a.5.9.)
                            PRISON, YPRES.
Main Dressing Station - BRANDHOEK (G.12.b.8.6.)
Regtl. Bearers supplemented by R.A.M.C. Bearers will clear **only** as far as Regtl. Aid Posts. Walking wounded will be guided by Directing Signs skirting N. and S. sides of YPRES to Corps Walking Wounded Collecting Station whence lorries will evacuate them to CCS.
   As the advance proceeds New Collecting Posts will be selected possibly at FREZENBERG and BRIDGE HOUSE and evacuation will take place from these points

P.T.O.

(4) REPORTING OF CASUALTIES.

(a) Company, Platoon and Section Commanders must take with them into action a roll of all N.C.Os. and men under their command. This will be carried in the right breast pocket so that in the event of a casualty, it is known where it can be found.

A Roll Call must be made as soon as possible after heavy fighting. Casualty reports are of two kinds :-

(a) Wires

    (1) Accurate daily casualty wire which must be rendered to Bn. H.Q. by 11 a.m.

    (2) Showing approximate casualties sustained during heavy fighting, and sent in addition to the accurate daily wire.

(b) Nominal Rolls. Showing killed, wounded, and missing, to be rendered as soon as possible after every engagement.

W.E.H. Rhein
Captain.,
Adjutant, 8th. R. Inniskilling Fusiliers..

Copy No. 1 to O.C. "A" Coy.
"   " 2 "   "   "B" "
"   " 3 "   "   "C" "
"   " 4 "   "   "D" "
"   " 5 .. Signalling Officer.
"   " 6 .. 2/Lieut. A.H. Borcherds.
"   " 7 .. Medical Officer.

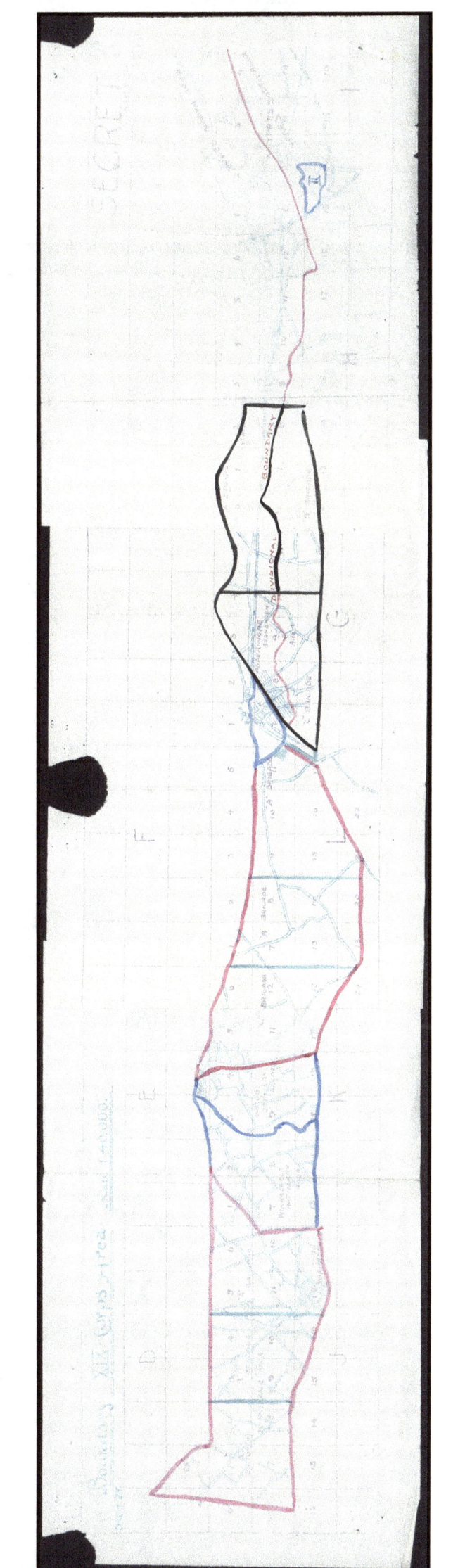

Secret.   S/329.

                    H.Q.
                      49th. I. B.

            Ref. Amendments to Special
        Administrative Instructions of 21. 7. 17
        Para 3 Line 4 – should not para .5
        read Para 3, please?

                                    T. Boardman
                            "Lieut.-Colonel, Commanding"
                            9th (S) Battalion R. Innis. Fusiliers.

        23. 7. 17

        Yes. Thanks.
                    K Bowen.

                                STAFF CAPTAIN
                                49th INFTY. BRIGADE.

        23.7.17

SECRET   Copy No......

49th INFANTRY BRIGADE.

SPECIAL ADMINISTRATIVE INSTRUCTION No. 10.

COLLECTION AND ESCORT OF PRISONERS OF WAR.

21-7-17.

1. The Corps cage will be at H.7.d.3.7.

2. The Right Divisional Cage will be at ECOLE I.9.c.5.2.
   The Left Divisional Cage will be near LA BRIQUE I.2.b.9.9.

3. The route for prisoners from the Right Divisional Cage to Corps Cage will be - Track S. of YPRES to CANAL BRIDGE I.13.c.7.5. - track through H.18.b. and c, H.17.b. and a, H.16.b., H.15.b. and a, H.8.d. and c, to H.7.d.

4. The route for prisoners from Left Divisional Cage to Corps Cage will be - via BRIDGE over CANAL at I.1.b. to Infantry track through H.12.b. and a, H.11.b. and a, H.10.b. and a, to VLAMERTINGHE, thence main POPERINGHE Road to H.8.a.5.7 through H.8.a. to H.7.d.

5. The representative of the A.P.M. at Divisional Cage will give a receipt to fighting troops for all prisoners taken over.

6. Fighting troops who capture prisoners are to immediately search all Officers and take away from them all documents, which are then to be placed in an empty sand-bag and sent with the escort to the Divisional Cage. Special attention should be paid to pockets in back skirt of tunics and back of trousers. Personal belongings and decorations should not be removed.

H. Bowen
Captain,
Staff Captain,
49th Infantry Brigade.

Issued as laid down in para 6, of S.A.I. No. 1 dated 3-7-17.

SECRET   Copy No......

49th INFANTRY BRIGADE.

SPECIAL ADMINISTRATIVE INSTRUCTION No. 11.
ORDNANCE SERVICES.

21-7-17.

1. During active operations units are frequently transferred from one formation to another. Efforts will be made by D.A.D.O.S. to ensure that there shall be as little interruption as possible in the supply of Ordnance Stores. He will establish communication with the incoming unit with a view to having its incomplete indents transferred and provisions made for its requirements. He should seek out the unit and not wait for the unit to come in search of him.

2. All Machine or Lewis Guns salved are to be taken to the Divisional Armourer's Shop for overhaul. Rifles, Lewis Gun Magazines etc., should be re-issued only after examination by an Armourer.

3. During an action, D.A.D.O.S. will maintain communication with the units of the Division, and will endeavour to see Quartermasters daily. He will be thus able to ascertain the immediate needs of units.

Bowen
Captain,
Staff Captain,
49th Infantry Brigade.

Issued as laid down in para 6 of S.A.I. No. 1 dated 3-7-17.

SECRET.   49th INFANTRY BRIGADE.   Copy No ......

SPECIAL ADMINISTRATIVE INSTRUCTION No. 12.

MARCH DISCIPLINE.

21-7-17.

1. The normal hourly halts are to be observed throughout a march, unless orders are given to the contrary.

2. Horsed vehicles of all kinds must keep to the RIGHT side of the road.

    Riding horses, during halts will be drawn up on the RIGHT side of the road, facing inwards.

3. Whenever columns of troops or vehicles halt, cross roads and road junctions must be left clear. When possible, heads of columns should be halted at least 50 yards short of cross roads and road junctions.

4. Whenever a road is not broad enough for three lines of traffic, vehicles whether halted or on the move, must leave a gap between each group of 6 to act as a "refuge" for single vehicles, and so enable meeting traffic to pass.

5. All ranks, mounted or dismounted, will march IN the column, and not abreast of it.

6. Details marching with transport will carry their arms and equipment and will march under proper command.

    The one man per vehicle told off to attend to the brakes, will march fully equipped immediately behind his vehicle.

    Cooks may put their packs only on the cooks wagon, but will otherwise march fully equipped.

7. No man except the driver will ride on any vehicle unless in possession of a written permit signed by an Officer.

8. The current days forage may be carried on vehicles. With this exception NOTHING BEYOND AUTHORISED LOADS OF VEHICLES IS TO BE CARRIED.

                                                     Captain,
                                              Staff Captain,
                                            49th Infantry Brigade.

Issued as laid down in para 6 of S.A.I. No. 1 d/ 3-7-17, and copies No. 15, 16, & 17, to 157th Coy. R.E., 114th Coy. A.S.C. and 113th Fd. Amb. respectively.

SECRET.   Copy No......

49th INFANTRY BRIGADE.

SPECIAL ADMINISTRATIVE INSTRUCTION No. 13.

VETERINARY ARRANGEMENTS.

21-7-17.

1. There will be a Veterinary Aid Post at H.11.b.9.9. (Sheet 28) to which units can take any animal for dressing, and where they can leave such animals as are unable to march to a Mobile Veterinary Section.

2. There will be a Mobile Veterinary Section at G.11.a.4.6. and one at G.14.b.5.4., and two others whose positions will be notified later.

3. In the event of a move forward the Veterinary Aid Post will be sent forward and a Mobile Veterinary Section will take its place.

4. A man of the Veterinary Aid Post will patrol the road daily between YPRES and VLAMERTINGHE to see that no injured animals are left on the road without attention.

5. Units who have them will make full use of their A.V.C. Sergeants who should see that injured animals of their unit are at once attended to, and if necessary handed in to the Veterinary Aid Post or a Mobile Veterinary Section.

H. Bowen.
Captain,
Staff Captain,
49th Infantry Brigade.

Issued as laid down in para 6 of S.A.I. No. 1 d/3-7-17, and copies No. 15, 16, and 17, to 157th Coy. R.E., 144th Coy. A.S. and 113th Fd. Amb. respectively.

SECRET   Copy No.......

49th INFANTRY BRIGADE.

SPECIAL ADMINISTRATIVE INSTRUCTIONS.

AMENDMENTS.

1. Reference S.A.I. No. 4 "BURIAL ORDERS", para 6, line 6. For "Corps G.R.U. Office" read "O.C. Graves Registration Unit of the Army".

2. Reference S.A.I. No. 7. "MEDICAL ARRANGEMENTS". para 4 line 3, for "lorries" read "busses".
    line 5, delete this line and substitute:-
    "busses will run up to H.12.c., on to KRUISSTRAAT and return via BELGIAN BATTERY CORNER. These busses will pick up walking wounded from Left Division on the main road near GOLDFISH CHATEAU and from the Right Division near BELGIAN BATTERY CORNER. Chief Engineer has also given permission for the returning road construction lorries to be used for conveyance of less severely wounded. These lorries will be running on "Z" day to near St. JEAN and POTIJZE CHATEAU."

    Para 5, line 6 - delete from "either" to "or" inclusive.

3. Reference S.A.I. No. 6 "WATER SUPPLY".
    para 1, add - "Tank No. 14.A. at H.2.d.8.3.(Sheet 28) yielding daily 3,200 gallons".

    Para 3. Under "Sheet 28" add -
        G.10.d.7.3.
        G.10.b.10.3.
        G.16.b.2.5.
        G.15.b.9.4.

                                            Bowen
                                            Captain,
                                            Staff Captain,
                                            49th Infantry Brigade.
21-7-17.

SECRET.   Copy No.... 5

49th INFANTRY BRIGADE.

SPECIAL ADMINISTRATIVE INSTRUCTION No. 9.
REINFORCEMENT DEPOT.

1. As previously notified the XIX Corps Reinforcement Depot will be established at MERCKEGHEM about 9 miles N. of St. OMER.

2. There will be a Commandant and Administrative Staff for the Camp and under him each Division will have a Depot Battalion; each Brigade a Depot Company; and each Battalion a Depot Platoon.

3. The following Staff has been selected for the 16th Div. Depot Battalion, and will be held in readiness:-

Commanding Officer	-	Major L.L. FARMER, 2/R. Irish Regt.
Adjutant & R.M.	-	Capt. C.E. JAMESON, 2/R. Dublin Fus.
Musketry Officer	-	Capt. T.H. CROFTON, 6th Connaught Rangers.
Medical Officer	-	Cap. A.J. LEWIS, R.A.M.C.
Sgt. Major.	-	As detailed by 47th Brigade.
Q.M.S.	"	" " " 48th Brigade.
Clerk	"	" " " Div. Emp. Coy.
Camp duties 18 O.R.	"	" " " " " "
2 Gas N.C.Os.	"	" " " Div. Gas Officer.
2 Bayonet Fighting Instructors	"	" " " 49th Brigade.
4 R.A.M.C.	"	" " " A.D.M.S.

For each Brigade Company.

	Off.	O.R.
Commanding Officer	1	
Other Officer	1	
Sgt. Major and Q.M.S.		1
Sgt. Instructor of Musketry		1
Platoon Commanders	4 (1 for each Battalion in Brigade).	

The personnel from this Brigade will be found as under:-

Commanding Officer	-	Capt. A.F. CODDINGTON. 7/8th R. Irish Fus.
Other Officer	"	2/R. Irish Regt.
Platoon Commanders	"	1 from each Battalion.
Sgt. Major and Q.M.S.	"	2/R. Irish Regt.
Sgt. Instructor of Musketry	"	7/R. Innis. Fus.
2 Bayonet Fighting Instructors	"	8/R. Innis. Fus. and 7/8th R. Irish Fus

4. Units will be administered for rations and Ordnance by the VIIIth Corps. All indents for rations and Ordnance will be sent through the Commandants Office.

5. The Reinforcement Railhead will be notified later. The Commandant will arrange for an Officer and guides and the necessary transport to meet all Reinforcements arriving.

6. If necessary the Division will advance funds for the purpose of buying the necessary utensils for Officers' and Sergeants' Messes.

7. Each Division will be responsible for providing their Depot Battalion with the necessary stationery required. The O.C. each Company must also be in possession of an imprest account for the payment of his men. Depot Battalions will correspond direct with their Divisions.

8. Frs. 500 will be put at the disposal of O.C. Depot Battalion for the provision of papers and games.

9. Reinforcements will not be sent up to units while in the line without the permission of the Corps. No Reinforcements will leave the Depot without the permission of the Corps having first been obtained.

10. Arrangements will be made by the Chemical Advisor, XIXth. Corps for instruction in the fitting of gas masks and instruction in the use of box respirators and P.H. Helmets.

11. The train service to and from WATTEN and POPERINGHE is as follows:-

Depart WATTEN 14.19 hrs., Arrive POPERINGHE 17.58 hrs.
Depart POPERINGHE 6.18 & 9.27 hrs, Arrive WATTEN 10.8 & 13.0 hrs.

2/Lieut.

17.7.17.

A/Staff Captain, 49th. Inf. Brigade.

"A" Form
MESSAGES AND SIGNALS.

Army Form C. 2121
(in Pads of 100).

TO: 7 Pl ... 2nd R. Ir. Regt.
8 Pl Lewis ... 7/8 Rl Ir Fus.

Sender's Number: SCC 620
Day of Month: 18th

AAA

The following were received from 16th Divn A. aaa

49th Bde will now furnish 4 NCOs as platoon commanders of Bde Coy instead of 4 officers as ordered aaa added 49th Inf Bde repeated 16th Div Depot Btn 19th Corps reinforcement Camp ends aaa.

Ref 49th L/Bde Special Administrative Instruction no 9. Batts will act in accordance with above wire.

From
Place: 49th Inf Bde.
Time:

73

49th.I.B. No.S.C.C.9/984

2nd.R.Irish Regt.
7th.R.Innis. Fus.
8th.R.Innis. Fus.
7/8th.R.Irish Fus.

With reference to Brigade Special Administrative Instruction No. 9.

All personnel for Reinforcement Camp other than advance party, who have already reported, will be held in readiness to proceed at short notice, probably on the 19th. inst.

17.7.17.

2/Lieut.
A/Staff Captain, 49th. Inf. Bde.

MESSAGES AND SIGNALS.

TO: ~~7th Rl Inniskilling~~
8th Rl Inniskilling Fus

Sender's Number.	Day of Month.	In reply to Number.	AAA
*SCC616	18th		

Ref 49th Bde Special Administrative Instructions No 9 aaa The 7th Rl Inniskilling Fus will find a Bayonet Fighting Instructor and the 8th Rl Inniskilling Fus the Instructor of Musketry.

13240 Sgt. J McEvor.

From Place: 49th Inf Bde

S E C R E T.   Copy No. 5

49th INFANTRY BRIGADE.
SPECIAL ADMINISTRATIVE INSTRUCTION No. 2

ORGANIZATION OF PACK TRANSPORT.

24-7-17.

1. The Brigade will organize a Pack Transport Company as under for use during an advance over ground impassable for wheeled vehicles. This Company will be organized at once; practice will take place once a week, by arranging for one unit at a time to draw their supplies from Supply Refilling Point and deliver same to Transport Lines by Pack Transport.

2. **Composition of Company.**

Animals.
- 6 Pack animals per Battn. — 24.
- 18 1st Line Transport animals per Battn. — 72.
- 16 animals from M.G. Coy. — 16

  112

Saddlery.
- 18 Pack Saddles per Battn. — 72.
- 6 Pack Saddles per Battn. are expected from Division.(if not received-Universal Saddles). — 24.
- 16 Pack Saddles from M.G. Coy. — 16

  112.

Men.
- 6 Pack Mule leaders per Battn. — 24.
- 2 Spare drivers per Battn. — 8.
- 16 1st Line Transport drivers per Battn. — 64.
- 16 Drivers M.G. Coy. — 16.

  112.

3. Lieut. H.F. Reid, 7/R. Innis. Fus., will command the Brigade Pack Transport Company.

4. The Company will be divided into five sections as follows:

"A" Section.   6 Pack animals.   ) From
               18 1st Line Transport Animals.) "A" Bn.

"B" Section.   As per "A" but provided from "B" Bn.

"C" Section.   As for "A" but provided from "C" Bn.

"D" Section.   As for "A" but provided from "D" Bn.

"E" Section.   M.G. Section of 16 animals.

Contd page 2.

para 4 Contd.

Each Section will be in charge of an Officer; "A", "B", "C", "D", under Battalion Transport Officers, "E" Section under M.G. Coy. Transport Officer.

5. One man must lead only one animal.

6. Water will be carried in petrol tins in special bags on pack saddles. <u>Care must be taken to bring back empty tins.</u> If this is not done the further supply of water after an initial issue has been made to Battalions is rendered :: extremely difficult, and almost impossible. A reserve of tins is to be carried on the water carts, from which deficiencies can be made up.

7. On the Brigade advancing to the attack the following loads will be carried:-

First Load. "A", "B", "C" and "D", Sections will each carry:-

```
7 animals - water - 8 tins each = 112 gallons.
4 animals - L.G.Drums - 32 each = 128 drums.
6 animals - S.A.A., rifle oil and flannelette
                                 = 12.000 etc.
7 animals - picks and shovels.
   ( 4 carrying 32 shovels each.       )=144
   ( 2    "     24 picks each.         )shovels.
   ( 1 carrying18 picks and 16 shovels)= 60 picks.
```

"E" Section.

Loads arranged by O.C. M.G. Coy.

Second Loads.

As directed by Battalion Commanders.

A total load of 200 lbs. per animal is not to be exceeded.

8. Every animal will carry head rope, nose bag, hay net and water bucket.

9. In addition to the Sections formed as detailed in para 4, each Battalion will organise an emergency pack section of 9 animals.

Brigade Headquarters will also organize an emergency pack section of 6 animals.

Contd page 3

3.

Para. 9 contd.

These emergency pack sections will be for use under the Quartermasters' of Units for the purpose of ration carrying, when the Brigade Pack Company is not available.

The Brigade Headquarters emergency section will carry rations and water.

H. Bowen.
Captain.
Staff Captain.
49th Infantry Brigade.

Issued as laid down in para 6 of S.A.I. No. 1.
Copy No. 10 to Lt. Reid, 7/R. Innis. Fus.
 "   " 16 " 1104 Coy A.S.C.

BILLETING LIST.

To accompany 49th Inf. Bde. Administrative Instruction No.13.

UNIT.	Map Reference.	O.	O.R.	Remarks.
2/R. Irish Regt.	L.7.d.7.5.	6	100	Mess, Office Transport.
	L.7.b.1.4.	-	155	
	L.7.a.9.6.	-	100	
	L.7.b.2.8.	1	100	Transport.
	L.7.b.6.5.	2	80	
	L.7.b.8.6.	1	40	
	L.7.a.2.5.	1	-	
	L.7.d.4.4.	1	-	
	L.7.d.5.1.	-	20	
7/R. Innis. Fus.	L.8.c.9.5.	-	20	H.Q.
	L.8.b.6.3.	4	30	
	L.8.a.9.7.	-	10	
	L.8.a.5.5.	3	40	Mess.
	L.8.c.3.5.	-	150	Office.
	L.8.c.6.6.	2	-	
	L.8.c.8.6.	4	-	
	L.8.d.3.8.	-	20	
	L.8.d.3.6.	-	10	
	L.8.d.3.7.	-	10	
	L.8.d.8.6.	1	40	Office.
	L.8.d.9.2.	1	125	Mess.
8/R. Innis. Fus.	L.13.c.4.4.	1	120	H.Q. and Mess.
	L.13.a.4.4.	5	50	Mess.
	L.13.a.7.8.	-	10	
	L.13.a.4.10.	-	25	
	L.13.b.2.6.	-	100	
	L.13.b.7.7.	-	40	
	L.13.b.8.6.	1	-	Mess.
	L.13.b.1.3.	1	-	
	L.13.d.6.3.	-	70	
7/8th R. Irish Fus.	L.14.b.8.4.	1	200	H.Q. & Transport
	L.14.a.2.0.	-	60	
	L.14.b.2.3.	-	30	
	L.14.b.9.3.	1	-	
	L.14.b.5.9.	-	25	
	L.14.c.8.8.	2	40	Mess.
	L.14.c.7.4.	-	10	
	L.14.d.1.8.	-	10	

It is pointed out that tents supplement the above accommodation.

S.E.C.R.E.T.   Copy No. 5

49th INFANTRY BRIGADE.

SPECIAL ADMINISTRATIVE INSTRUCTIONS No. 8.

POLICE ARRANGEMENTS FOR STRAGGLER POSTS.

25-7-17.

1. A Brigade line of Straggler Posts will be established under orders to be issued later.

2. The line of the YSER CANAL has been taken as the Divisional line by the Corps which are on our right and left. In order to conform to this, it has been decided:-

   (a) To guard all entrances to YPRES; these posts will be under the control of the Town Major.
   (b) To guard the bridges of the Canal; these posts will be under the control of the A.P.Ms. of the Divisions concerned.

   The posts in detail are:-

No.1.	Position.	M.P.	O.R.	By Whom Found.
1.	Canal Bridge I.I.b.6.4.	1	3	Left Division.
2.	Road at I.1.c.2.3.	1	3	"
3.	Bridge 9. I.7.a.8.3.	1	3	Town Major YPRES.
4.	Bridge 10.I.7.c.4.8.	1	3	" " "
5.	Bridge 13.I.13.a.9.3.	1	3	" " "
6.	Sally Post.I.14.a.6.2.	1	3	" " "
7.	LILLE Gate.I.14.a.9.2.	1	3	" " "
8.	Sally Post.I.14.b.1.6.	1	3	" " "
10.	Menin Gate. I.8.b.1.1.	1	3	" " "
11.	Thourout or South Gate.	1	3	" " "
12.	Dixmude or North Gate	1	3	" " "
13.	Bridge 7.I.1.d.4.5.	1	3	" " "
14.	Bridge 1.14.c.7.6. Approx.	1	3	Right Division.

   The left Straggler Post of II Corps is at I.19.b.1.9.

   The Right Strong Point of XVIII Corps is at I.1.b.7.7.

3. Divisional Collecting Posts will be situated as follows:-

   (a) Right Division at BELGIAN Battery Corner,H.24.a.4.9.
   (b) YPRES at the Prison YPRES.
   (c) Left Division at H.9.a.2.9. on the main POPERINGHE Road.

4. The strength of Divisional Straggler Collecting Posts will not be less than 1 Sgt. M.M.P.,and 6 Regimental Police. The A.P.M. will issue orders to all Divisional Straggler Posts and to the Divisional Collecting Post.

2.

Straggler Posts Contd.

5. Arrangements will be made by A.P.M. to collect Stragglers at least once daily, as opportunity occurs from the Town Major YPRES whose Collecting Post is given in (b) of para 3 above.

6. The following will be included in the equipment of all Straggler Posts.- Lamp, Drinking Water stoved in - petrol tins, spare gas helmets, Iron Rations, Field Dressings, picks and shovels, sandbags, empty S.A.A. boxes for Grenades. At Divisional Straggler Collecting Station there will be rather a larger supply of the above in order to replenish the forward posts if necessary, also means of giving a hot meal to Stragglers before returning them to 1st Line Transports.

Bowen
Captain,
Staff Captain,
49th Infantry Brigade.

para 6 of
Issued as laid down in/S.A.I. No.1 of 3-7-17.

SECRET.   Copy No. ..5..

19th INFANTRY BRIGADE

APPENDIX "A" TO SPECIAL ADMINISTRATIVE INSTRUCTION No. 3.

Reference para 2 of above Instruction the following will probably be the location of the Division in the BRANDHOEK AREA.

UNIT.	LOCATION.	REMARKS.
Divl. H.Q.)	POPERINGHE.	
R.A.)	Rue de YPRES	
C.R.E.)	Transport at G.7.b.8.6.	
D.A.D.O.S.	POPERINGHE.	

BRANDHOEK No. 1 AREA.

"A" Bde.H.Q.	H.2.c.3.7. Red Rose Camp.	Huts.
A. Battn.	H.1.b.8.0. " " "	"
B. "	H.1.a.8.0. Derby Camp.	Tents.
C. "	G.6.a.2.2. Query Camp.	"
D. "	G.6.d.4.4. "B" Camp.	Huts & Tents.
M.G. Coy.	G.6.b.2.0. Bedouin Camp.	Tents.
T.M. Bty.	G.6.d.4.4. "B" Camp.	"
Bde. Tpt. Lines.	G.4.c.1.8.	

BRANDHOEK No. 2. AREA.

"B" Bde. H.Q.	H.7.a.1.1.	Huts.
A. Battn.	G.11.c.6.6. St. Lawrence Camp.	"
B. Battn.	G.11.c.6.6. Erie Camp.	"
C. "	G.18.a.6.5. Toronto Camp	Huts and Tents
D. "	G.18.a.6.5. " "	"
M.G. Coy.	G.11.c.6.6. St.Lawrence Camp.	"
T.M. Bty.	G.18.a.6.5. Toronto Camp.	Tents.

Transport Lines at Camps with unit.

BRANDHOEK No. 3. AREA.

"C" Bde. H.Q.	16 Rue de Boeschepe POPERINGHE.	
A. Battn.	G.16.a.9.5.	Tents.
B. "	G.15.a.0.1.	"
C. "	G.9.a.2.4.	"
D. "	~~G.11.a.5.8.~~ G 14 a 1.5	"
M.G. Coy.	G.8.b.3.1.	"
T.M. Bty.	G.8.b.3.1.	"

Transport Lines at Camps with unit.

Pioneer Battn.	H.7.c.6.3.	
3 Field Coys	~~Crosses~~ G 11 d.1.5	And Transport.
Divl. Train.	G.15.a.8.5.	H.Q. Coy. (No.1.Coy.
	G.15.a.5.2.	(No.2. Coy. (No.3.Coy.
Mob. Vet'y. Sect.	G.14.b.3.5.	21th 15th Div. Mob. Sect.

Bowen
Captain,
Staff Captain,
19th Infantry Brigade.

23-7-17.

Issued as laid down in para 6 of S.A.I. No. 1. dated 3-7-17-
Copies No. 15, 16, & 17, to 157th.Coy.R.E., 144th.Coy.A.S.C. and 113th Field Amb. respectively.

S E C R E T   Copy No. 5

49th INFANTRY BRIGADE.

SPECIAL ADMINISTRATIVE INSTRUCTIONS.

AMENDMENTS.

28.7.17.

1.Appendix "A" to S.A.I. No. 3.

BRANDHOEK No. 3 AREA - "D" Battalion for "G.14.a.5.8." read "G.14.a.1.5"

3 Field Companies - For "G.11.d.2.8." read "G.11.d.1.5"

Bowen.
Captain.
Staff Captain.
49th Infantry Brigade.

Issued as laid down in para 6 of S.A.I. No. 1. dated 3.7.17. copies 15, 16, 17, to 157th Coy. R.E., 144th Coy. A.S.C., and 153th Fd. Ambulance respectively.

SECRET. Copy No. 6.

49th INFANTRY BRIGADE.

ADMINISTRATIVE INSTRUCTIONS No. 13.

Reference 49th Infantry Brigade Order No. 144 d/22.7.17.

1. The advance parties of units mentioned in para 2 of the above order should proceed early on the morning of the 25th inst. and get a thorough knowledge of the billet to be occupied by their unit.
   A suitable place for one of their number to meet his unit on the morning of the 26th inst. and guide it to its billets appears to be the Cross Roads in K.12.c.
   Units billeting accommodation will be as approximately shown in the attached list, though this is by no means to be taken as definate.

2. **Water.** Wells exist at:-

   L.14.a.3.1.   L.14.c.5.2.   L.13.c.4.4.
   L.13.c.3.1.   L.1.d.0.0.

   Horse troughs at L.7.a.7.3.   L.7.b.5.0.
   L.7.c.7.6.   L.14.b.3.4.
   L.13.d.3.4.   L.7.b.2.8.

3. Supply Railhead for the 49th Brigade Group on the 26th inst., will be WIPPENHOEK (L.28.c). and refilling point will be L.9.b.2.4. Supply wagons to march empty to this new refilling point.

4. Lorries are available for the move as follows, and there are no limits as to the number of trips to be made by them. 1 for each Battalion 1 for Bde. H.Q. M.G. Coy. and T.M. Bty. 1 guide from each Battalion, 1 from M.G. Coy. and 1 from T.M. Battery will report to Staff Captain at 9.45 p.m. on the evening of 25th July, at Brigade H.Q. in order to conduct lorry allotted to where required.

5. All units will send in to Brigade Headquarters by 6 p.m. 27th inst., a list giving map references of their billets and tents occupied giving accommodation etc., and numbers of tents; transport lines are also to be given.

6. All billets and Transport Lines in this area are to be left   scrupulously clean.

Captain.
Staff Captain.
49th Infantry Brigade.

24.7.17.

Copies to -
No. 1. G.O.C.
2. Brigade Major.
3. Asst. Staff Captain.
4. 2/R. Irish Regt.
5. 7/R. Innis. Fus.
6. 8/R. Innis. Fus.
7. 7/8th R. Irish Fus.
8. M.G. Coy.
9. T.M. Battery.
10. 144th Coy. A.S.C.
11. 157th Coy. R.E.
12. 113th Field Ambulance.
13. File.

Cancel 49th Infantry Brigade Special Administrative Instruction No. 6, 6A, and 6B, for which the attached S.A.I. No. 6 is substituted.

[Stamp: 8TH (S) BATTALION, S/608, 26 JUL. 1917, R. INNISS. FUSILIERS.]

25-7-17

Captain,
Staff Captain,
49th Infantry Brigade.

Issued as laid down in para. 6 of S.A.I. No. 1. copies 15, 16, and 17 to 157th Coy. R.E., 144th Coy. A.S.C., and 113th Fd. Amb., respectively.

SECRET.   Copy No....

49th INFANTRY BRIGADE.

SPECIAL ADMINISTRATIVE INSTRUCTION. No. 6.

WATER SUPPLY.

1. **WATER SUPPLY EAST OF POPERINGHE.**

    The initial water points in the forward area for the supply of drinking water are located as follows:- (Sheet 28). Water carts, water tank lorries, and water bottles will be able to refill at these points.

Tank	No. 4.	at	G.7.d.9.5.	yielding daily	7.400	galls:
"	" 5.	"	G.3.c.7.3.	"	25.250	"
"	" 6.	"	G.15.b.2.6.	"	11.700	"
"	" 9.	"	H.14.a.9.6.	"	7.000	"
"	" 11.	"	G.10.c.4.9.	"	15.500	"
"	" 14.	"	H.8.b.9.9.	"	5.000	"
"	" 14A.	"	H.2.d.8.3.	"	3.200	"
"	" 14B.	"	H.3.c.2.5.	"	3.200	"
"	" 32.	"	G.12.c.5.1.	"	4.000	"
"	" 48	"	G.12.a.9.9.	"	5.000	"

2. (a) The first Forward Water Point will be established for operations just off the road West of existing pumping house near the Swimming Bath in the N.E. corner of YPRES.

    (b) It is hoped to establish the Second Forward Water Point on the SAINT JEAN - WIELTJE Road, W. of WIELTJE.

    (c) Tank lorries, water carts, and water bottles will be able to be filled at both refilling points when completed.

3. As soon as tanks are established at the Second Forward Water Point the tank lorries will fill at the Initial Water Points and fill the tanks at the Second Forward Water Point. As soon as this has been done, water carts and water bottles can be filled from the Second Forward Water Point. Until then, water carts will fill at Initial Water Points or First Forward Water Point.

Contd. page 2.

4. As soon as the Second Forward Water Point is completed the tank lorries will work forward to a Third Forward Water Point.

5. HORSE WATER SUPPLY is from existing streams and ponds, long shallow wells dug by units themselves, from wells completed by R.E., and from tank supply.

The location of the shallow wells are :-

BRANDHOEK AREA No. 1.

G.5.c.4.9.   G.10.b.1.4.
G.5.d.4.7.   G.11.a.8.3.
G.6.c.4.2.
G.12.a.9.9.   H.7.a.4.5.

BRANDHOEK AREA No. 2.

G.10.d.1.2.   G.10.d.7.3.   G.10.b.10.3.
G.11.d.6.1.   G.11.d.5.9.   G.12.c.8.5.
G.12.b.8.8.   G.12.d.7.4.   G.16.b.2.5.
G.17.a.7.7.   G.17.a.5.7.   G.18.a.4.6.
G.12.d.5.3.   H.7.b.3.3.

BRANDHOEK AREA No. 3.

G.3.d.2.8.   G.3.c.4.8.   G.4.c.1.9.
G.9.a.8.4.   G.9.b.1.5.   G.9.c.4.4.
G.9.d.3.4.   G.10.c.2.2.   G.14.a.1.6.
G.14.b.5.6.   G.15.a.3.3.   G.15.b.9.4.
G.15.b.2.9.

The wells will be fitted with pumps and troughs and can water 40 horses at a time. The location of horse water tanks are:-

BRANDHOEK AREA No 2.   - G.17.b.8.6.
"   "   "   - G.12.c.8.4.

6. **WATER SUPPLY WEST OF POPERINGHE.**

No. 74 Water Point for water bottles, water carts and tank lorries is at L.11.a.6.5.

7. Lorry-fed reservoirs have been built at L.17.d.10.4. in WATOU AREA No. 2. and at J.10.b.2.3. in WINNEZEELE AREA No. 2. These will be kept filled by the Section of No. 8 Water Column.

Contd. page 3.

3.

8. Shallow wells have been sunk as under:-

WATOU AREA No. 1.

L.10.b.3.6.   L.11.c.8.1.   L.17.a.7.5.

WATOU AREA No. 2.

L.1.c.3.2.   L.7.a.7.3.   L.7.d.3.3.
L.7.b.5.0.   L.7.c.7.6.   L.14.c.5.2.

WATOU AREA No. 3.

K.5.b.1.5.   K.5.d.5.2.   K.17.b.2.1.
K.11.a.7.3. K.12.d.2.1.
K.18.b.0.4. K.5.d.3.2.

WINNEZEELE AREA No. 1.

J.11.c.3.4.   J.12.b.8.5.   J.18.b.9.2.
J.18.b.9.8.

WINNEZEELE AREA No. 2.

J.4.d.7.5.   J.10.d.1.6.

WINNEZEELE AREA No. 3.

N I L.

9. (a) Horses are not to be watered direct from reservoir tanks or pits. Divisions will erect sufficient watering troughs in the vicinity of horse lines into which the water is to be pumped.

(b) An Officer, or, in exceptional cases when no Officer is available, a Warrant Officer or Senior N.C.O. will be in charge of every watering parade. Men are to dismount when horses are being watered and bits removed.

(c) Watering troughs will be so arranged that horses are not taken along or across main roads to water. Horses are not to be taken to water along tram lines, railway lines, or through fields where railway lines are in process of construction.

Horses are not to be allowed to drink until water troughs are full.

Contd. page 4.

4.

10. Water wardens are to be placed in charge of each point, wells, and set of water troughs by the unit in whose area they are situated.

The duties of water wardens are as follows:-

(a) Be responsible for the water pipes and tanks at his stand, the supervision of the issues of water there, and see that there is no waste.

(b) He will keep a daily record of all issues.

(c) He will report to Brigade Headquarters (Staff Captain) water carts parading at the tanks without necessary water details or a sufficient supply of chloride of lime in proper containers.

(d) He will see that water is properly chlorinated, and should keep a supply of chloride of lime at the tank.

(e) Any damage, leakage etc, at tank stands or water pipes will be reported to Brigade H.Q. (Staff Captain).

(f) He will be responsible that water is properly turned off before leaving post.

(g) He will carry out instructions by O.C. Sanitary Section, as regards any sanitary measures.

11. In the event of an advance all sources of drinking water must be tested before use by the Medical Officer of units. Sentries and warning notices must be posted on suspected water supplies and samples sent in at once to the nearest Mobile Laboratory for conformation. Notice boards labelled (a) DRINKABLE or (b) POISONOUS will be erected at all sources of water supply tested during an advance.

H J Bowen

25-7-17.

Captain,
Staff Captain,
49th Infantry Brigade.

Issued as laid down in para 6 of S.A.I. No. 1 dated 3-7-17 and copies No. 15, 16, and 17 to 157th Coy. R.E., 144th Coy. A.S.C., and 113th Field Ambulance respectively.

S E C R E T.　　　　　　　　　　　　　　COPY NO... 5.

49th INFANTRY BRIGADE.

APPENDIX "A".
TO
SPECIAL ADMINISTRATIVE INSTRUCTION No. 10.

ORDERS FOR GUARDS OVER PRISONERS OF WAR.

1. Guards are warned against allowing slightest loophole for escape. If a prisoner of war manages to escape those responsible will be very severely dealt with.

2. Guards are forbidden to converse with prisoners either by talking or by signs.

3. No one will be allowed to enter the cage or hold conversation with any prisoner of war except the Provost Marshall Staff, Staff Officers, Intelligence Officers and Officers in charge of prisoners.

4. It is forbidden for any one to give anything or take anything whatsoever from prisoners of war, except as may be required by the Intelligence.

5. Prisoners will receive ordinary rations.

6. After examination, prisoners will be kept separate from those about to be examined.

7. Special attention is to be paid to Officer prisoners as they are more likely

　　(a) to endeavour to escape.
　　(b) to influence their men.

They should be kept separate from the men.

8. N.C.Os should also be kept apart and in small groups if possible.

9. No smoking is to be allowed.

10. If any prisoner gives trouble, they will be placed apart from the others and handcuffed.

11. If any prisoners of war are allowed out of the cage for work, to draw water, to go to the latrines, or for any other purpose, they will always have an armed escort.

P.T.O.

2.

12. Prisoners will keep their places clean. Rations will be issued to them on parade. They will do their own cooking if any is wanted.

13. In the case of large numbers, they will be frequently counted.

14. A receipt will always be given for the number of prisoners taken over, and for the number of prisoners handed over. Before the receipt is given prisoners are to be carefully counted.

15. Prisoners will be warned that any one resisting an escort, or attempting to escape, will be instantly shot.

N. Bowen.
Captain.
Staff Captain.
26.7.17.   49th Infantry Brigade.

Issued as laid down in para 6 of S.A.I. No.1. dated 3.7.17.

S E C R E T.   Copy No... 5.

49th INFANTRY BRIGADE.

APPENDIX "B".

to

SPECIAL ADMINISTRATIVE INSTRUCTION No. 10.

ORDERS FOR OFFICERS OR N.C.Os IN COMMAND OF
ESCORTS TO PRISONERS OF WAR.

1. Prisoners are to be counted before being taken over, and a receipt given for them on A.F.W. 3443. Prisoners are also to be counted after halted.

2. When prisoners of war are handed over a receipt must be obtained for them on A.F., W. 3443.

3. When on the march the escort should be in strength at the rear of the column, the flanks being lightly guarded.

4. Rifles of escort should be loaded. Any prisoner who attempts to escape should be shot. The escort should on no account be allowed to scatter in pursuit.

5. When halted, neither Officers, N.C.Os soldiers or civilians are to be allowed to crowd around prisoners they must be kept at a distance. No one is allowed to talk to the prisoners on the line of march, nor at any other time except -

    Staff Officers.
    A.P.M.
    Intelligence Officers.
    Officers in charge of prisoners.

6. Escorts are not to take buttons, caps or other articles from prisoners, neither may they give prisoners food or tobacco, ar. llow civilians or soldiers to give them anything.

7.

P.T.O.

7. Officer prisoners will be kept separate from the men, and should be closely watched, by an Officer or N.C.O. who should march immediately behind them. N.C.Os should also be kept apart when possible.

8. Any prisoners who have been examined by Intelligence Officers should be kept separate from those who have not.

9. Keep a sharp look-out for any prisoners attempting to get rid of papers when on the march. Any papers thrown away by prisoners to be collected and handed to the Intelligence Officer.

H. Bowen.
Captain.
Staff Captain.
29.7.17. 49th Infantry Brigade.

Issued as laid down in para 6 of S.A.I. No.1. dated 3.7.17.

S E C R E T.   Copy No. 5

49th INFANTRY BRIGADE.

SPECIAL ADMINISTRATIVE INSTRUCTION No. 8. (Part 2).

26.7.17.

1. In the event of an advance in which the 16th Division takes part it may be necessary to form Battle Straggler Posts in front of those provided by the 15th Division which are on the line of the Canal. The probable lines would be either:-

   (a) POTIJZE (I.4.a.3.0) to HELL FIRE CORNER (I.10.c.9.8)

   or

   (b) CAMBRIDGE ROAD I.5.a.5.8. to I.11.b.3.5.

2. If (a) line is adopted 3 posts would be required:-

   I.14.a.3.0.   I.10.c.9.8.   I.10.c.9.3.

   If (b) line, then 2 only would be required:-

   I.5.a.5.8.   I.11.b.3.5.

3. Each post will consist of 1 N.C.O. and 3 O.R. reinforced by 1 M.M.P. The personnel of these posts will be found as follows and should be earmarked accordingly:-

   Brigade in Reserve - 3 N.C.Os and 9 O.R.
   A.P.M. - 3 M.M.P.

   The Infantry personnel will be called for by A.P.M. at short notice.

                                                Captain.
                                             Staff Captain.
                                          49th Infantry Brigade.

Issued as laid down in para 6 of S.A.I. No. 1.
dated 3.7.17.

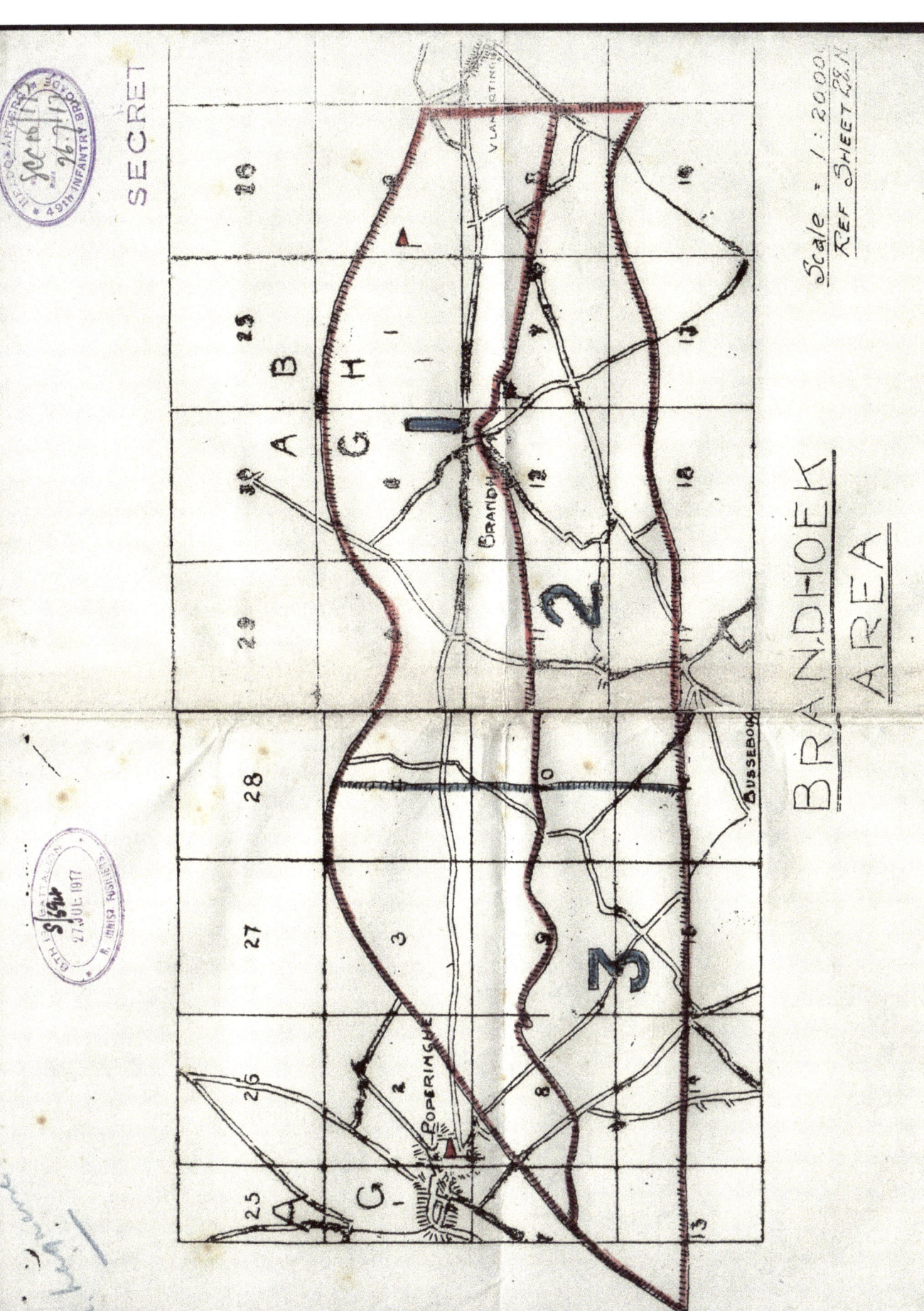

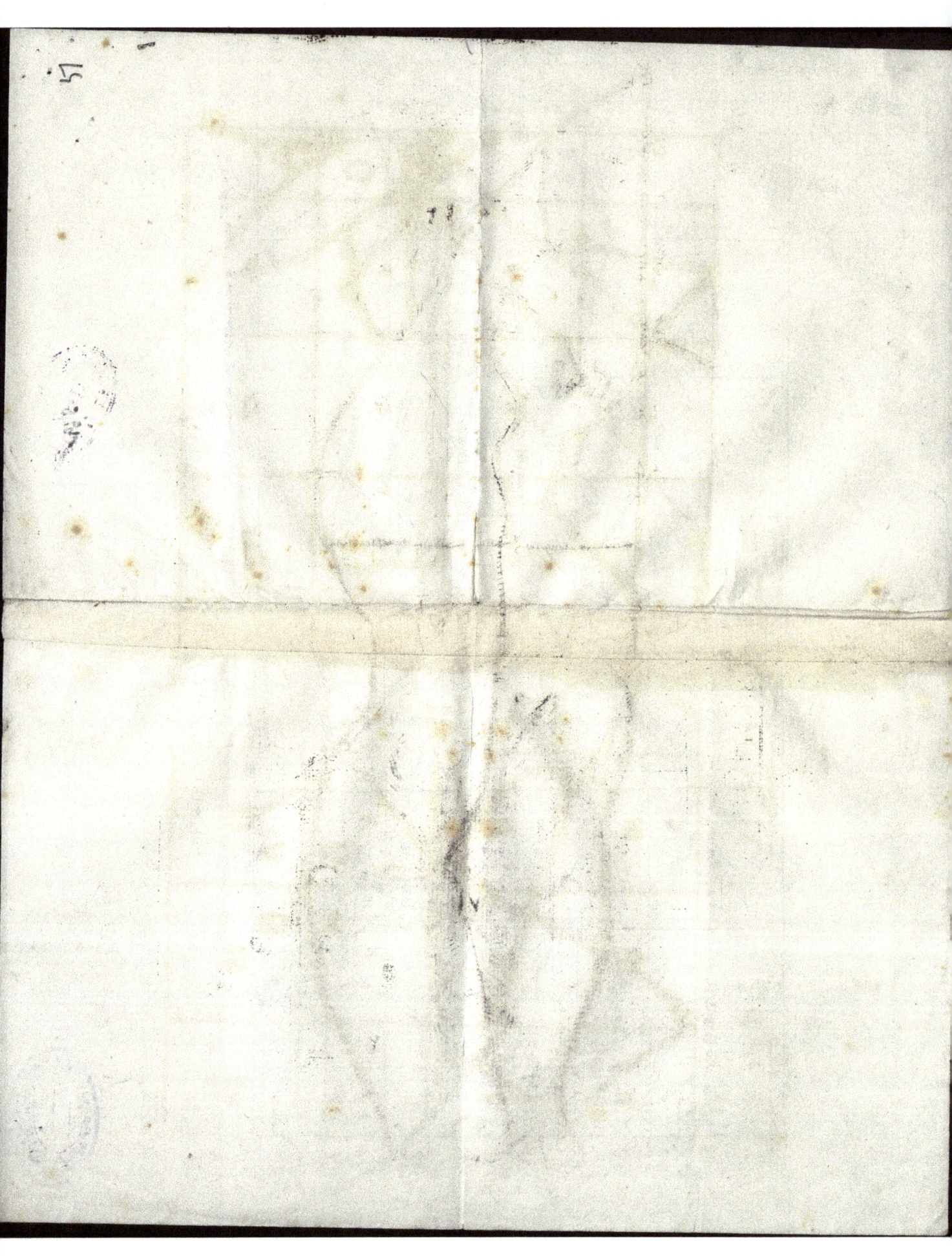

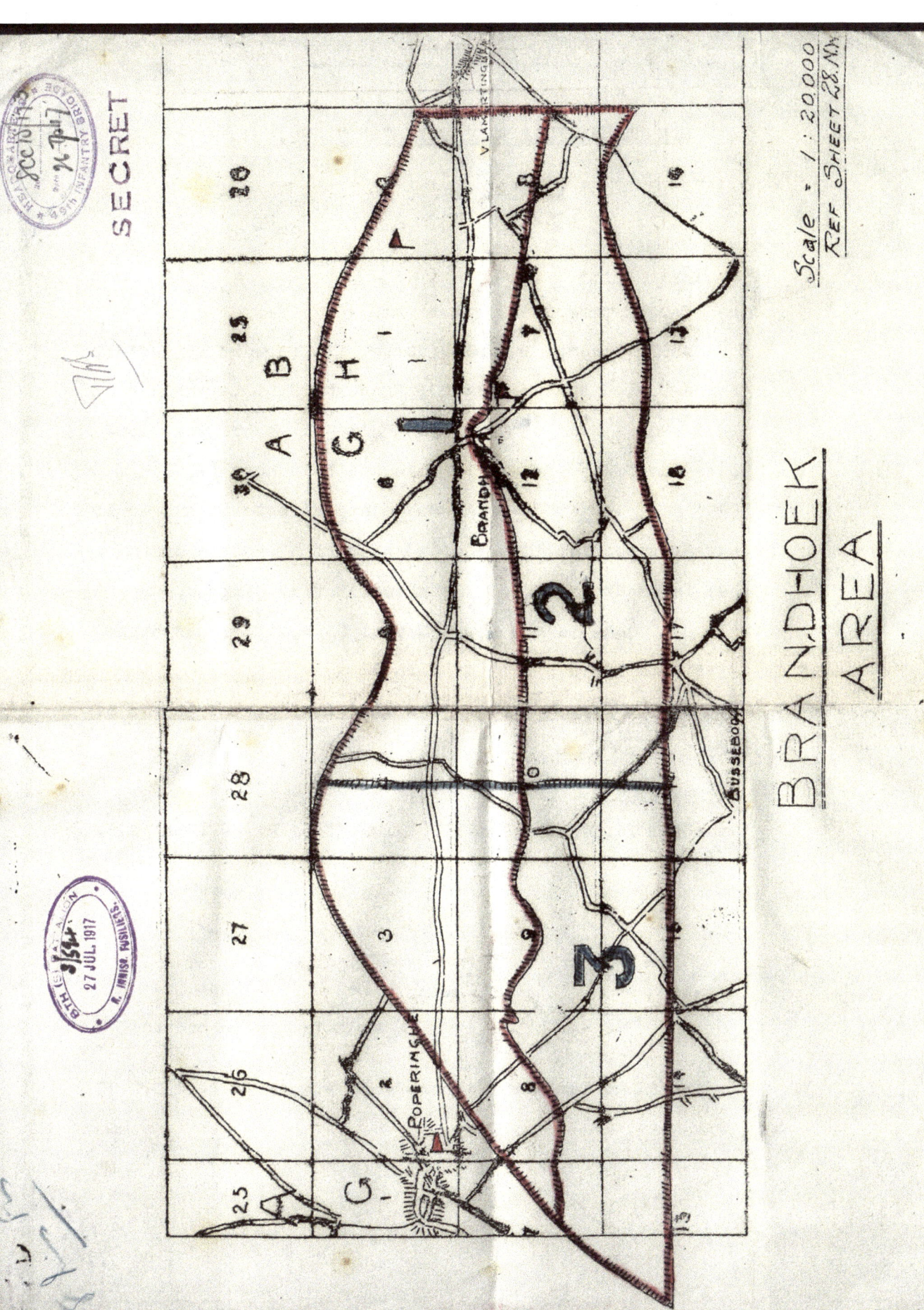

S E C R E T.   Copy No... 5 52

49th INFANTRY BRIGADE.

SPECIAL ADMINISTRATIVE INSTRUCTIONS.

AMENDMENTS.

26.7.17.

1. <u>S.A.I. No.4.</u>

   (a) Cancel para 5 and substitute:-

   "5. The Divisional Burial Officer will forward all effects of men buried by him to the Brigade or Unit to which the deceased men belong. The Unit will thereupon complete the necessary certificate and Inventory (A.F.,N. 3190) and place them with each man's effects in the small bags provided for that purpose, labelling and returning them in sandbags to the Divisional Burial Officer, who will send them to the Corps Burial Officer for despatch by rail to D.A.G., 3rd. Echelon."

   (b) Delete from "together" in line 4 of para 7 to end of para.

2. <u>S.A.I. No.8.</u> Add "(Part I)" to end of Title.

   i.e. "SPECIAL ADMINISTRATIVE INSTRUCTION No. 8 (Part I)".

                                              [signed] Bowen
                                                   Captain.
                                                Staff Captain,
                                              49th Infantry Brigade.

Issued as laid down in para 6 of S.A.I. No.1. d/3.7.17.

S E C R E T. 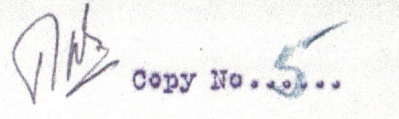 Copy No. 5

49th INFANTRY BRIGADE.

SPECIAL ADMINISTRATIVE INSTRUCTIONS.

AMENDMENT.

29.7.17.

1. S.A.I. No. 6 "WATER SUPPLY" renumber para 7 as "7 A".

Insert new para:-

"7.B. - Two sterilizing lorries have been allotted for back areas, and will be stationed in the WATOU ARTILLERY AREA at K.3.c1.1. and in the WINNEZEELE No. 3 AREA at J.1.b.2.3.

Water carts are to draw from these sterilizers in preference to reservoirs mentioned in para "7 A".

Bowen
Captain.
Staff Captain.
49th Infantry Brigade.

Issued as laid down in para 6 of S.A.I. No. 1. dated 3.7.17. Copies No. 15, 16, and 17 to 157th Coy. R.E. 144th Coy. A.S.C., and 113th Fd. Ambulance respectively.

S E C R E T. Copy No. 5

49th INFANTRY BRIGADE.

SPECIAL ADMINISTRATIVE INSTRUCTION.

AMENDMENT.

1. S.A.I. No. 14 "REPORTING OF CASUALTIES".

Cancel para 3b, and substitute:-

"(b) The phase which commenced at MIDNIGHT 25/26th July, will close and a new phase will begin at MIDNIGHT 8/9th August. Approximate wires will commence "Total Estimated Casualties from 9th August."

7-8-17

Bowen.
Captain,
Staff Captain,
49th Infantry Brigade.

Issued as laid down in para 6 of S.A.I. No. 1 dated 3-7-17.

SECRET.   Copy No. **5**..

49th INFANTRY BRIGADE.

SPECIAL ADMINISTRATIVE INSTRUCTION. No. 14.

REPORTING OF CASUALTIES.

(Refers also to pages 39 and 40 of Fifth Army General Circular Memorandum No. 1).

29.7.17.

1. Company, Platoon, and Section Commanders must take with them into action a roll of all N.C.Os and men under their command. This will be carried in the right breast pocket in order that, in the event of a casualty, it is known where it can be found.

    A roll call should be made as soon as soon as possible after heavy fighting.

2. Casualty reports are of two kinds; (a) Casualty wires (b) nominal rolls.

    (a) **CASUALTY WIRES.**
    - (1) **Accurate daily wire** - sent at a fixed hour whether fighting is in progress or not.
    - (2) **Approximate (or estimated) wire** - showing approximate casualties sustained during heavy fighting, and sent in <u>addition to the accurate daily wire</u>.

    (b) **NOMINAL ROLLS.** Showing killed, wounded, and missing. These are sent by units with their A.F., B. 213 (Strength Return).

APPROXIMATE CASUALTY WIRES.
(Not to effect the sending of the Accurate Daily wire).

3. (a) Approximate (or estimated) casualties will be reported in "phases", and each wire will include all casualties since the commencement of the "phase", whether previously reported on an accurate daily wire, approximate wire, or not at all. In other words, during any "phase" each wire is cumulative and includes all losses since the

Commencement/

commencement of that "phase", and under no circumstances will the word "Additional" be used.

(b) The "phase" commenced at MIDNIGHT 25/26th July and approximate wires will commence "Total estimated casualties from 26th July", until the commencement of a later "phase" is notified, when the date is amended as necessary.

4. (a) No distinction is drawn <u>in approximate wires</u> between killed, wounded and missing.

(b) The words "Officers" and "Other Ranks" will not be used; the two categories being separated by the word "and".
e.g. "2 and 49" means "2 Officers and 49 O.R."
"4 and nil" means "4 Officers and no O.R."
(c) The prescribed code names of units will be used.

5. Every effort should be made to send an approximate casualty wire so as to reach Bde. H.Q. by 5 p.m. each evening. If further heavy casualties occur during the night another wire should be sent so as to reach Brigade H.Q. by 9 a.m.

MISCELLANEOUS.

6. <u>"Missing" Casualties.</u> - (a) When 50 or more of any one unit are reported "missing" in an accurate daily wire, a brief statement should be sent <u>with</u> the wire (or directly after by D.R.L.S.) of the circumstances under which they became "missing". Casualty wires must not be delayed if this report is not to hand.

(b) When personnel are reported as "missing" and are afterwards accounted for, this information should be forwarded as soon as possible so that reports may be rectified.

7. <u>Casualties "Attached".</u> When reporting casualties among men attached to a unit it should always be stated in the wire if the unit to which the attached men belong has been informed.

8. For the purposes of accurate casualty wire - "killed" includes all those who died before they have been taken over by the medical authorities.

If the/

If the latter take over a case alive, the return should be "wounded". Should death take place subsequently it is the duty of the Medical Authorities to report the fact.

The expression "Died of Wounds" or "since died of wounds" should not appear in a casualty wire.

Bowen.
Captain.
Staff Captain.
49th Infantry Brigade.

Issued as laid down in para 6 of S.A.I. No. 1. dated 3.7.17.

Sent copy No 17 to 113 Fd. Amb.

S E C R E T. Copy No........

5th. R. Innis. Fus. S/539 - 30-7-17.

ADMINISTRATIVE INSTRUCTIONS.

The following extracts from 49th. Infantry Brigade Special Administrative Instructions are published for the information and guidance of all Officers :

(1) BURIAL ARRANGEMENTS. During heavy fighting a Divisional Burial Section will be maintained - Strength 1 Officer and about 23 Other Ranks. This Section will be reinforced by personnel detailed by Corps Labour Troops. This section is intended to assist Infantry Units in the burial of their dead in the event of heavy casualties, and it will work behind a line defined by D.H.Q. from time to time.
All Officers who are in charge of burial parties should note the following instructions :-
(1) Remove nothing from dead until placed in grave.
(2) Bury British, French and German Dead separately.
(3) Mark flanks of graves with posts - if available wire.
(4) Enter map references and nearest land mark in note book.
(5) Select unexposed position.
(6) Bury Officers with men.
(7) Enter particulars as body placed in grave.
(8) Tie up personnel belongings with identity cord; place in bag, write particulars on label.
    Separate sandbags to be kept for each nationality.
(9) Mark graves with cross, and serial number.

Return of en buried in all cases to be rendered to Battn. H.Q. giving the following information :-
(a) No. Rank. Name and initials. (c) By whom buried.
(b) Bn., Regt., and exact place of burial. (d) Identification number.

(2) PRISONERS OF WAR.
(a) The Right Divisional Cage will be at ECOLE I.9.c.5.2.
(b) The representative of the A.P.M. will give a receipt on A.F.W. 3443 to fighting troops for all prisoners taken over.
(c) Fighting troops who capture prisoners are immediately to search all Officers, and take away from them all documents which are then placed in an empty sandbags and sent with escort to the Divisional Cage. Special attention should be paid to pockets in back skirt of tunics and back of trousers. Personnel belongings and decorations should not be removed.
(d) Rifles of escorts should be loaded and any prisoners attempting to escape should be shot. Escorts must on no account scatter in pursuit.

(3) MEDICAL ARRANGEMENTS. Right Division.
Regtl. Aid Posts - Two behind CAMBRIDGE ROAD.
Collecting Stations - MENIN Road I.9.d.4.6.
                     POTIJZE CHATEAU
Advanced Dressing Stations - KRUISSTRAAT (H.24.a.5.9.)
                             PRISON, YPRES.
Main Dressing Station - BRANDHOEK (G.12.b.8.6.)
Regtl. Bearers supplemented by R.A.M.C. Bearers will clear only as far as Regtl. Aid Posts. Walking wounded will be guided by Directing Signs skirting N. and S. sides of YPRES to Corps Walking Wounded Collecting Station whence lorries will evacuate them to CCS.
As the advance proceeds New Collecting Posts will be selected possibly at FREZENBERG and BRIDGE HOUSE and evacuation will take place from these points

P. T. O.

(4) REPORTING OF CASUALTIES.

(a) Company, Platoon and Section Commanders must take with them into action a roll of all N.C.Os. and men under their command. This will be carried in the right breast pocket so that in the event of a casualty, it is known where it can be found.

A Roll Call must be made as soon as possible after heavy fighting. Casualty reports are of two kinds :-

(a) Wires
    (1) Accurate daily casualty wire which must be rendered to Bn. H.Q. by 11 a.m.
    (2) Showing approximate casualties sustained during heavy fighting, and sent in addition to the accurate daily wire.

(b) Nominal Rolls. Showing killed, wounded, and missing, to be rendered as soon as possible after every engagement.

W.E.H. Ennis

Captain.,

Adjutant, 8th. R. Inniskilling Fusiliers..

Copy No. 1 to O.C. "A" Coy.
" " 2 " " "B" "
" " 3 " " "C" "
" " 4 " " "D" "
" " 5 .. Signalling Officer.
" " 6 .. 2/Lieut. A.H. Borcherds.
" " 7 .. Medical Officer.

SECRET.   Copy No.........

8th. R. Innis. Fus. S/539 - 30-7-17.

ADMINISTRATIVE INSTRUCTIONS.

The following extracts from 49th. Infantry Brigade Special Administrative Instructions are published for the information and guidance of all Officers :

(1) <u>BURIAL ARRANGEMENTS.</u> During heavy fighting a Divisional Burial Section will be maintained - Strength 1 Officer and about 23 Other Ranks. This Section will be reinforced by personnel detailed by Corps Labour Troops. This section is intended to <u>assist</u> Infantry Units in the burial of their dead in the event of heavy casualties, and it will work behind a line defined by D.H.Q. from time to time.

All Officers who are in charge of burial parties should note the following instructions :-
   (1) Remove nothing from dead until placed in grave.
   (2) Bury British, French and German Dead separately.
   (3) Mark flanks of graves with posts - if available wire
   (4) Enter map references and nearest land mark in note book.
   (5) Select unexposed position.
   (6) Bury Officers with men.
   (7) Enter particulars as body placed in grave.
   (8) Tie up personnel belongings with identity cord; place in bag, write particulars on label.
      Separate sandbags to be kept for each nationality.
   (9) Mark graves with cross, and serial number.

Return of men buried in all cases to be rendered to Battn. H.Q. giving the following information :-
(a) No. Rank. Name and initials.   (c) By Whom buried.
(b) Bn., Regt., and exact place of burial. (d) Identification number.

(2) <u>PRISONERS OF WAR.</u>
   (a) The Right Divisional Cage will be at ECOLE I.9.c.5.2.
   (b) The representative of the A.P.M. will give a receipt on A.F.W. 3443 to fighting troops for all prisoners taken over.
   (c) Fighting troops who capture prisoners are immediately to search all Officers, and take away from them all documents which are then placed in an empty sandbags and sent with escort to the Divisional Cage. Special attention should be paid to pockets in back skirt of tunics and back of trousers. Personnel belongings and decorations should not be removed.
   (d) Rifles of escorts should be loaded and any prisoners attempting to escape should be shot. Escorts must on no account scatter in pursuit.

(3) <u>MEDICAL ARRANGEMENTS.</u> Right Division.
Regtl. Aid Posts - Two behind CAMBRIDGE ROAD.
Collecting Stations - MENIN Road I.9.d.4.6.
               POTIJZE CHATEAU
Advanced Dressing Stations - KRUISSTRAAT (H.24.a.5.9.)
               PRISON, YPRES.
Main Dressing Station - BRANDHOEK (G.12.b.6.6.)
Regtl. Bearers supplemented by R.A.M.C. Bearers will clear <u>only</u> as far as Regtl. Aid Posts. Walking wounded will be guided by Directing Signs skirting N. and S. sides of YPRES to Corps Walking Wounded Collecting Station whence lorries will evacuate them to CCS.
As the advance proceeds New Collecting Posts will be selected possibly at FREZENBERG and BRIDGE HOUSE and evacuation will take place from these points

                                                  P. T. O.

(4) REPORTING OF CASUALTIES.

(a) Company, Platoon and Section Commanders must take with them into action a roll of all N.C.Os. and men under their command. This will be carried in the right breast pocket so that in the event of a casualty, it is known where it can be found.

A Roll Call must be made as soon as possible after heavy fighting. Casualty reports are of two kinds :-

(a) Wires
    (1) Accurate daily casualty wire which must be rendered to Bn. H.Q. by 11 a.m.
    (2) Showing approximate casualties sustained during heavy fighting, and sent in addition to the accurate daily wire.

(b)   Nominal Rolls. Showing killed, wounded, and missing, to be rendered as soon as possible after every engagement.

Captain.,

Adjutant, 8th. R. Inniskilling Fusiliers..

```
Copy No. 1 to O.C. "A" Coy.
 "   "  2 "   "   "B"  "
 "   "  3 "   "   "C"  "
 "   "  4 "   "   "D"  "
 "   "  5 "  Signalling Officer.
 "   "  6 "  2/Lieut. A.H. Borcherds.
 "   "  7 "  Medical Officer.
```

SECRET.   Copy No..5..

49th INFANTRY BRIGADE.

APPENDIX "A" to

SPECIAL ADMINISTRATIVE INSTRUCTIONS No. 4.

1. It is to be clearly understood that the primary duty of burial of the dead falls on the unit and the Brigade concerned.

   Corps and Divisional Burial parties are only to supplement and assist the units and to guard against the exceptional cases, when circumstances prevent the units from carrying out of the duty.

2. CEMETERIES EAST and WEST of YPRES:-

MENIN Road South	I.9.d.2.5.	(Sheet 28.)
PRISON, YPRES	I.7.b.1.5.	" "
ASYLUM, YPRES	H.12.d.9.7.	" "
ST. JEAN, White House.	I.3.a.8.6.	" "
POTIJZE	I.4.c.2.9.	" "

MENDINGHEM Siding (No. 46 C.C.S.)	E.6.d.1.9.	(Sht.27)
VLAMERTINGHE Military Cemetery	H.3.c.3.3.	" 28
VLAMERTINGHE Hopstone	H.2.c.4.4.	" "
BRANDHOEK Military Cemetery	G.12.b.8.5.	" "
POPERINGHE Military Cemetery	G.8.c.8.4.	" "

                                              Captain.
                                              Staff Captain.
   31.7.17.   49th Infantry Brigade.

   Issued as laid down in para 6 of S.A.I. No. 1. dated 3.7.17.

SECRET.   Copy No. 5

49th INFANTRY BRIGADE.

APPENDIX "A" to
SPECIAL ADMINISTRATIVE INSTRUCTIONS No.7.

1. If the necessity arises, (and the tactical situation permits) Infantry Brigades will be called upon to furnish parties of Infantry Stretcher Bearers to supplement the Divisional Medical Services.

2. These parties will be organised as follows:-

   (a) As far as possible they will be composed of drummers and pipers of units.

   (b) Each Brigade party will consist of 1 Officer and 50 men furnished by -

   2/R. Irish Regt.   13 O.R.
   7/R. Innis. Fus.   1 Off and 12 O.R.
   8/R. Innis. Fus.   13 O.R.
   7/8th R. Irish Fus.   12 O.R.

   Personnel as above will be earmarked and held ready by units to be provided when asked for.

3. "Bearers Assembly Points at Advanced Dressing Stations or Collecting Posts will be selected and communicated to all concerned.
   At these points "S.B." Armlets, Stretchers, First Field Dressings and a supply of drinking water will be dumped.

4. Under orders from the Divisional Headquarters this auxiliary bearer party will be sent to the Officer Commanding Advanced Dressing Station or Collecting Station at the nearest Bearer Assembly Point.
   At these points the men will pile their arms and stack all surplus equipment, taking over "S.B." Armlets, one stretcher per four men and First Field Dressings on a scale of three per man. Water bottles will be filled and carried for use by the wounded.

P.T.O.

2.

Par 4 Contd.

This Auxiliary Bearer Party will then work under under its own officer as directed by O.C. Advanced Dressing Station or Collecting Post concerned. On completion of duty they will return all Ambulance Equipment to the Bearer Assembly Points, and take over their own arms and equipment before proceeding to rejoin their units.

R. Bowen
Captain.
Staff Captain.
31.7.17.   49th Infantry Brigade.

Issued as laid down in para 6 of S.A.I. No. 1, dated 3.7.17.

2nd R. Irish Regt.
7th R. Innis Fus.
8th R. Innis Fus.
7/8th R. Irish Fus.
49th M.G. Company.
49th T.M. Battery.

S E C R E T.
* * * * *

49th Inf. Bde. No. S.S. 47 - 19-7-17.

Herewith copies of B. A. B. Trench Code No. 3 (and 16th Div. Letter giving corrected number) issued as under :-

2nd R. Irish Regt.   (5 copies) Nos 11428 - 11432.
7th R. Innis Fus.   (5 copies) Nos 11433 - 11437.
8th R. Innis Fus.   (5 copies) Nos 11438 - 11442.
7/8th R. Irish Fus. (5 copies) Nos 11443 - 11447.
49th M.G. Company   (3 copies) Nos 11448 - 11450.
49th T.M. Battery   (2 copies) Nos 11451 - 11452.

Please acknowledge receipt.

Major,
for Brigade Major, 49th Infantry Brigade.

S E C R E T.

2nd R. Irish Regt.
7th R. Innis Fus.
8th R. Innis Fus.
7/8th R. Irish Fus.

49th Inf. Bde. No. XXM.S.S.47/2 - 21-7-17.

    Herewith 3 extra copies of B.A.B. Trench Code No. 3 for issue to Signal, Transport and Intelligence Officers respectively :-

2nd R. Irish Regt.	Nos. 11513 -	11515.
7th R. Innis Fus.	Nos. 11516 -	11518.
8th R. Innis Fus.	Nos. 11519 -	11521.
7/8th R. Irish Fus.	Nos. 11522 -	11524.

ACKNOWLEDGE.

Major,
Intelligence Officer, 49th Infantry Brigade.

SECRET. S/327/1
O. C.
"A" Coy.

Herewith copy No. 11438
of B.A.B. Trench Code No. 3.,
and 16th. Div. letter giving
corrected number.
Please acknowledge without delay
delay.

W. E. H. Rivis
Captain.,
Adjutant, 8th. R. Innis. Fusrs.,
20 /7/ 17.

The Adjt.
Received.

20/7/17

"B" Coy.

Herewith copy No. 11439 of B.A.B. Trench Code No. 3., and 16th. Div. letter giving corrected number.

Please acknowledge without delay. delay.

W.E.H. Innis
Captain.,
Adjutant, 8th. R. Innis. Fusrs.,
20/7/17.

The Adjutant.
Above received
please

W Russell Maynard
Capt
O.C. B Coy

20-7-17
7-35 PM

To
adjutant

SECRET.   S/327/1

O. C.
"D" Coy.
_____

Herewith copy No. 11441
of B.A.B. Trench Code No. 3.,
and 16th. Div. letter giving
corrected number.
Please acknowledge without delay
delay.

W.E.H. Orr(?)
Captain.,
Adjutant, 8th. R. Innis. Fusrs..
20 /7/ 17.

To Adjutant

Received the above

20/7/1917

H. Broadley Capt
O.C D. Coy

Secret.

S/328/1.

Lieut. W. F. Ellis M.C.
            Signalling Off.

Herewith B.A.B. French Code No 3
Copy No 11519 together with 16th Div.
letter giving corrective numbers.

    Please acknowledge receipt
hereon without delay

                    W. E. H. Muir
                    "Capt. & Adjutant."
23. 7. 17   8th (S) Battalion R. Innis. Fusiliers.

To The Adjutant
8th Ry Innis Fus
Received B A B French Code
No 3 copy No 11519
            W F Ellis Lt
            o/c HQRS

Secret   S/328/1.

2/Lt. K.M. Borchards.

Herewith B.A.B. French Code No 3
Copy No. 11520, together with 16th Div
letter giving correction numbers

Please acknowledge receipt
hereon without delay.

W.E.H. Mair
"Capt. & Adjutant."
8th (S) Battalion R. Innis. Fusiliers.

23. 7. '17.

The Adjt.

+ letter
received.

B.A.B. Code Book 11520.

K.M.Borchards
2/Lt

23/7/17.

69

To Adjutant

B.A.B. code copy no 11440 received.

23/7/17.

H.W. Martin Capt
O.C. C Coy.

SECRET.

G. O. C.
2nd R.Irish Regt.
7th R. Innis Fus.
8th R. Innis Fus.
7/8th R.Irish Fus.
49th M.G.Company.
49th T.M.Battery.
157th Field Coy, R.E.
Staff Captain.
Bde. Intelligence Officer.
Bde. Signal Officer.
16th Div. (G).

49th Inf. Bde. No. S.O. 100 - 21-7-17.

      Herewith Copy No........3..... of 49TH INFANTRY BRIGADE INSTRUCTIONS FOR THE OFFENSIVE (INSTRUCTIONS Nos. 1, 2, 3 and 4).

      Please acknowledge receipt.

                                                           Captain,
                Brigade Major, 49th Infantry Brigade.

49th I.B.No.S.O.100.
22-7-17.

SECRET.

Copy No ......3...

49TH INFANTRY BRIGADE INSTRUCTIONS FOR THE OFFENSIVE.

INSTRUCTION NO. 1.

GENERAL PLAN AND PRELIMINARY DISPOSITIONS.

1. Offensive operations on a large scale, in which the XIXth Corps is to take part will shortly commence.

2. ENEMY DISPOSITIONS.

The German Lines opposite the XIXth Corps Front are held by one regiment of the 17th Division from about 100 yards South of the YPRES - ROULERS railway to about C.29.d.2.9, and one regiment of the 233rd Division from about C.29.d.2.9 to about C.29.b.6.1.

Each regiment has one battalion in the front system, one battalion in the STUEZPUNKT Line and one battalion in the GHELUVELT - LANGEMARCK Line. Each Division, in addition to two regiments disposed as above, has one regiment in Reserve.

3. GENERAL PLAN OF ATTACK:

(a) The attack will take place on "Z" day; the exact time and date will be notified later. It will be preceded by an Artillery Bombardment of some day's duration.

(b) The attack will be carried out in three stages as under :-

1st Objective.

To capture and consolidate the enemy's front system of trenches up to, and including, the BLUE LINE.

2nd Objective.

To capture and consolidate the enemy's second line system of trenches (STUTZPUNKT LINE) up to, and including, the BLACK LINE.

3rd (Final) Objective.

To capture and consolidate the enemy's 3rd Line System (GHELUVELT - LANGEMARCK)LINE) up to and including THE GREEN LINE.

The various objectives, and the times of leaving them, are shown on the attached map "A".

4. DISPOSITIONS FOR THE ATTACK.

(a). The XIXth Corps is to attack on a front of about 2,800 yards, with the 15th Division on the right, the 55th Division on the left and the 16th and 36th Divisions in Corps Reserve.

The frontage and objectives of the two attacking Divisions are shown on Map "A". Each of these Divisions will deliver the first assault with two Brigades in the front line and one Brigade in Reserve.

(b) The IInd Corps will be attacking on the right of the XIX Corps. Its left attack will be delivered by the 8th Division supported by the 25th Division.

(c) The XVIIIth Corps will be attacking on the left of the XIXth Corps. Its right attack will be delivered by the 39th Division, the 11th and 48th Divisions being in Reserve.

5. SITUATION OF DIVISION AT ZERO.

On Y/Z night the 16th Division (less Divisional Artillery and certain other units) will be disposed as follows in the BRANDHOEK Area :-

Div. H.Q.	POPERINGHE (G.1.d.5.1).
48th Inf. Bde.	"B" Bde. (or Southern) Area.
	Bde. H.Q. at BRANDHOEK (H.7.a.2.1).
49th Inf. Bde.	"A" Bde. (or Northern) Area.
	Bde. H.Q. at "A" Camp (H.2.c.2.7).
47th Inf. Bde.	"C" Bde. (or Western) Area.
Bde. H.Q.	POPERINGHE (G.2.c.2.2).

The Boundaries and accommodation of the above Areas are given in 49th Inf. Bde. ADMINISTRATIVE INSTRUCTION No. 3.

6. ACTION AT ZERO.

At Zero the 48th Inf. Bde. and the 155th Field Coy, R.E. will move forward from the BRANDHOEK Area to an Assembly Area in H.10 and H.16, where they will be in Corps Reserve and ready to move at 1 hours notice.

The remainder of the 16th Division in the BRANDHOEK Area will be held in readiness to move at 2 hours notice.

7. PROBABLE ROLE OF DIVISION.

As far as possible the 16th Division will be used to support the 15th Division.

When the 16th Division finally relieves the 15th Division the 48th and 49th Inf. Bdes. with their affiliated R.E. Companies will relieve the right and left sections of the 15th Division respectively. The 47th Inf. Bde. and the 156th Field Coy, R.E. will be in Reserve.

8. DISPOSITIONS OF 15TH DIVISION AT ZERO.

At Zero Hour the dispositions of the 15th Division will be as follows :-

(a) 15th Div. H.Q.   H.7.c.9.5.

(b) 44th Inf. Bde. H.Q.   I.4.d.6.0.

     44th Inf. Bde. Front. I.11.b.6.6 to I.5.b.3.0.

(c) 46th Inf. Bde. H.Q.   I.5.a.1.7.

   Right Battalion on front   I.5.b.3.0 - I.5.b.0.6.

   Left Battalion on Front.   I.5.b.0.6 - C.29.c.7.8.

   Support Battalion CAMBRIDGE TRENCH and ST. JAMES' TRENCH.

   Reserve Battalion HALF MOON TRENCH and West of it.

(d) 45th Inf. Bde. H.Q.   I.8.d.2.6.

   3 Battalions H.17.c., H.16.c., and H.16.d.

   1 Battalion H.17.a.1.9.

   Copies of a map (15th Div. Map No. 2, Scale 1/10,000), showing the trench system at present held by the 15th Division and the overland tracks that are in course of construction have already been issued to all concerned.

9. 15th DIVISION PLAN OF ATTACK.

   The 15th Division will attack with the 44th Inf. Bde. on the right, the 46th Inf. Bde. on the left and the 45th Inf. Bde. in reserve. The two leading Brigades will capture the BLUE and BLACK LINES, the dividing line between them being from I.5.b.3.0 to D.25.c.9.7.

   At Zero Hour the 45th Inf. Bde. will advance by the roads and tracks passing South of YPRES to a position of assembly West of the CAMBRIDGE ROAD. From here it will subsequently advance and capture and consolidate the GREEN LINE

10. DISPOSITIONS OF DIVISIONS ON FLANKS OF THE 15TH DIVISION.

   (a) 8th Division on Right.

   (b) 55th Division on Left.

11. ARTILLERY.

   (a) The Field Artillery supporting the attack of the 15th Division will consist of :-

   (i) Right Sub-Group.

      70th Bde. R.F.A.
      71st Bde. R.F.A.

   The Right Sub-Group will cover the front of the 44th Inf. Bde.

   (ii) Left Sub-Group.

      177th Bde. R.F.A.
      180th Bde. R.F.A.

   The Left Sub-Group will cover the front of the 46th Inf. Bde.

   (iii) Reserve Sub-Group.

      One Army Bde. R.F.A.

   The Reserve Sub-Group will assist in the barrages.

   (iv) Special Sub-Group.

      180th Army Bde. R.F.A.

   The Special Sub-Group will be used for Smoke Barrages, etc.

(b)   Heavy Artillery will also support the Division.

(c)   The Creeping Barrage will open at Zero on the enemy's front line. It will lift off the front line at Zero plus 6 minutes and will then move forward at an average rate of 100 yards in 4 minutes. It will remain stationary 300 yards beyond both the BLUE and BLACK LINE until the hour fixed for the advance from each line. There will be a protective barrage for one hour in front of GREEN LINE. At the end of this time the Barrage programme will come to an end.

(d)   In case of an S.O.S. Signal being received the batteries concerned will fire on their S.O.S. lines for ten minutes and cease fire at the end of this period unless the signal is repeated or orders are received from their respective Divisions or the B.G., H.A.

(e)   As soon as the BLACK LINE has been captured three F.A. Brigades per Division will begin to advance to positions in the vicinity of "No Man's Land".
    When the infantry advance from the BLACK LINE takes place other F.A. Brigades will advance to positions from which they can cover troops holding the GREEN LINE.
    Subsequently the whole of the Artillery will be moved forward to positions from which it will be able to support a further advance at an early date:

Captain,
Brigade Major, 49th Infantry Brigade.

22nd June 1917.

S E C R E T.   Copy No. 3

49TH INFANTRY BRIGADE INSTRUCTIONS FOR THE OFFENSIVE.

INSTRUCTION NO. 2.

TRAFFIC ARRANGEMENTS IN THE FORWARD AREA.

1. The attached Map shows :-

    A. The various tracks that have been prepared.

    B. The roads and traffic circuits that will eventually come into use.

A. COMMUNICATION TRENCHES.

2. There are four main communication trenches in the 15th Division Sector.

EAST and WEST LANES	OUT.
PICCADILLY	IN.
HAYMARKET	IN.
CURZON STREET	OUT.

    After Zero Hour PICCADILLY and HAYMARKET will if necessary be carried forward by the 15th Divisional Engineers so as to join up with ICE and IBERIA LANES in the present German Lines.

B. TRACKS.

3. Five tracks (Nos. 1 to 5), commencing in the neighbourhood of the MENIN and DIXMUDE GATES, have been carried forward as far as CAMBRIDGE TRENCH and OXFORD ROAD.

    There are also two tracks ("C" and "F") which might be used as alternative routes to the GORDON'S TRACK road for bringing up infantry should the latter road be subjected to heavy shelling. These two tracks are not passable by wheeled traffic and would be difficult, even for infantry, after heavy rain.

    The above tracks are marked on the ground but should be reconnoitred before troops are taken along them. This is especially the case as regards "C" and "F" Tracks.

2.

After Zero Hour the following tracks will be carried forward into the captured positions :-

(a) By 15th Divisional Engineers.

Two tracks wide enough for guns and horsed transport

(i) From I.5.d.5.4 through BILL COTTAGE and D.26.a.7.4 to BOSTIN FARM.
To be marked with white posts marked with one stroke.

(ii) From I.5.b.1.4 through BAVARIA HOUSE to DELVA FARM.
To be marked with white posts marked with two strokes.

(b) By 55th Divisional Engineers.

(i) No. 5 track (for Pack Transport) to be carried forward from OXFORD ROAD to the BLUE, and subsequently the BLACK LINE.

(ii) Two other forward tracks will also be marked out.

C. ROADS AND TRAFFIC CIRCUITS.

4. (a) After Zero Hour the Circuits on forward roads, together with others further east, will gradually come into force as the necessary repairs are completed.

(b) Pending the issue of further instructions the following have been issued by 15th Division :-

(i) The POTIJZE - YPRES road may be used as a forward road for clearing existing dumps.

(ii) Vehicles are not to halt on the YPRES - POTIJZE road.

They will draw off the road if a halt is required.

5. At 5 p.m. on "Z" plus 1 day further instructions as to Traffic circuits will come into force. A map showing these further circuits will be issued later to all concerned.

23rd June 1917.

Captain,
Brigade Major, 49th Infantry Brigade.

49th I.B. No. S.C.C. 2//28

2/R. Irish Regt.
8/R. Innis. Fus.

The G.O.C. directs that your unit be completely refitted with ammunition etc., as laid down in "49th Inf. Brigade Instructions for the Offensive No. 3". as early as possible.

You will therefore require to draw from Main Divisional Ammunition Dump at H.7.d.6.9.

To save delay, the annexed "authority to draw" is forwarded, which you are to attach to your indent on the Officer i/c of the Dump mentioned above.

Completed
10/8/17

K. Bowen.
Captain,
Staff Captain,
49th Infantry Brigade.

8-8-17.

SECRET Copy No ...3...

49TH INFANTRY BRIGADE INSTRUCTIONS FOR THE OFFENSIVE.

INSTRUCTION No. 3.

DRESS.

The following dress will be worn by all ranks during the forthcoming operations :-

Fighting Order.

(a) Clothing, arms and entrenching tools as issued.

(b) Equipment as issued. Either packs or haversacks worn on the back. If the pack is worn the haversack will not be carried.

(c) Box Respirators and P.H.Helmets.

(d) Iron Rations, unexpended portion of the day's rations, mess tin and cover, Field Dressing.

(e) Waterproof Sheets.

(f) Riflemen 170 rounds S.A.A., 2 Mills Bombs.

(g) Lewis Gunners 50 rounds S.A.A., 4 Lewis Gun Drums.

(h) Bombers 100 rounds S.A.A., 6 Mills Bombs.

(i) Rifle Bombers, 100 rounds S.A.A., 6 Rifle Grenades.

(j) Signallers, 50 rounds S.A.A.

(k) The personnel of Coy. and Platoon H.Q. will carry 50 rounds S.A.A. and 18 "P" Bombs. The "P" Bombs to be distributed as Company Commanders think fit.

(l) Personnel of Battalion and Coy. H.Q. will carry Very Pistols and ammunition and 6 S.O.S. Rifle Grenades per Headquarters.

(m) Every man will carry 2 sandbags.

All Officers will wear men's equipment and will carry Map, Binoculars, Prismatic Compass and Watch.

Captain,
Brigade Major, 49th Infantry Brigade.

23rd July 1917.

S E C R E T.   Copy No. 3

49TH INFANTRY BRIGADE INSTRUCTIONS FOR THE OFFENSIVE.

INSTRUCTION No. 4.

ENGINEER WORK AND CONSOLIDATION.

1. The following arrangements for Engineer Work and consolidation have been made by the two attacking Divisions.

   15TH DIVISION.

   (a) Infantry Brigades are responsible for the consolidation of objectives gained.

   (b) Captured Engineer Material is to be utilized in the consolidation of the position and information where it is to be found is to be given to Battalions by R.E. personnel carrying out the reconnaissances.

   (c) After the capture of the GREEN LINE an R.E. Stores Dump will be established as far forward as possible. When the position of this dump has been decided, the C.R.E. will inform Infantry Brigades.

   (d) The following work will be carried out under C.R.E's orders :-

   (i) Open up the POTIJZE - FREZENBERG road, making it fit for artillery and limbered wagons.

   (ii) Open up the two forward tracks mentioned in 49th Inf. Bde. INSTRUCTION No. 2.

   (iii) If required to do so, prolong PICCADILLY and HAYMARKET TRENCHES to join up with ICE and IBERIA LANES.

   (iv) Construct Strong Points at the following places :-

   D.26.a.7.2.
   D.20.c.7.2.
   D.20.a.5.9.

   55TH DIVISION.

   (e) The following work will be carried out by the 55th Divisional Engineers and Pioneers.

(i) Open up the SAINT JEAN - GREVENSTAFEL road.

(ii) Carry forward No. 5 track from OXFORD ROAD to the BLACK LINE.

(iii) Mark out two other forward tracks.

(iv) Construct Supporting Points (as distinguished from Strong Points made by the Infantry) at about the following places :-

        C.18.c.50.85.
        C.24.a.90.60.
        D.19.c.05.60.
        D.7.d.65.50.
        D.7.d.60.20.
        D.13.b.75.00.
        D.14.c.55.20.

The garrison of each of these Supporting Points will be 1 Machine Gun, 1 Lewis Gun and ½ Platoon of Infantry.

J.W.W.William, Captain,

24th July 1917.   Brigade Major, 49th Inf. Brigade.

2nd R. Irish Regt.
7th R. Innis Fus.
8th R. Innis Fus.
7/8th R. Irish Fus.
49th M.G. Company.
49th T.M. Battery.

SECRET.

49th Inf. Bde. No. S.O. 100/1 - 26-7-17.

With reference to 49TH INFANTRY BRIGADE INSTRUCTIONS FOR THE OFFENSIVE, INSTRUCTION No. 1, para 5, and INSTRUCTION No. 2. The attached Map shows the location of units at Zero, tracks and traffic circuits.

Please ACKNOWLEDGE.

Captain,
Brigade Major, 49th Infantry Brigade.

FOLLOWING DUMPS WILL BE FORMED BY 15TH. DIVISION.

No. on map.	Name.	Position.	Contents.
1	Q.A.A.	H.7.d.6.9.	Explosives, Lights.
2	Q.A.B.	I.3.d.4.4.	do.
3	A.R.A.	I.10.a.4.3.	do.
4	A.R.A.	I.9.d.3.8.	do.
5	A.R.B.	I.5.d.7.0.	do.
6	A.R.C.	I.6.c.9.7.	do.
7	A.R.D.	J.1.a.central	do.
8	M.V.A.	I.4.a.7.0.	do.
9	M.V.B.	I.5.a.4.1.	do.
10	M.V.C.	I.5.a.3.4.	do.
11	M.V.D.	C.30.c.9.7.	do.
12	B.M.D.	In H.17	S.A.A. Grenades & T.M. Ammn.
13	C.A.A.	I.5.d.2.2.	S.A.A., Grenades, T.M.Ammn. Revolvr. Ammn. Lights, explosives, rifle oil & flannelette.
14	C.A.B.	I.6.b.3.8.	S.A.A. & Grenades.
15	C.A.C.	D.25.c.8.5.	S.A.A. Grenades, Stokes Ammn. & Revolvr. Ammn.
16	C.A.D.	D.19.d.1.3.	S.A.A. Grenades & Stokes Ammn.
17	C.A.E.	D.20.a.9.3.	S.A.A. Gdes. Stokes Ammn. & Revolvr. Ammn.

SECRET.

G.O.C.
2nd R.Irish Regt.
7th R. Innis Fus.
8th R. Innis Fus.
6/8th R.Irish Fus.
49th M.G.Company.
49th T.M.Battery.
157th Field Coy, R.E.
Staff Captain.
Bde. Intelligence Officer.
Bde. Signal Officer.
16th Div. (G).

49th Inf. Bde. No. S.G. 100/2 - 26-7-17.

Herewith Copy No ....4.. of 49TH INFANTRY BRIGADE INSTRUCTIONS FOR THE OFFENSIVE (INSTRUCTION No. 5).

Please acknowledge receipt.

Captain,
Brigade Major, 49th Infantry Brigade.

SECRET.   Copy No ...4... 82

49TH INFANTRY BRIGADE INSTRUCTIONS FOR THE OFFENSIVE.

INSTRUCTION No. 5.

(1). General.

The main principles laid down in S.S. 148 "Forward Intercommunication in battle" will be followed in the coming operations with the following exceptions :-

(a) Each Artillery Brigade or Group will arrange to carry forward one line from cable head for the use of its F.O.O. O.C. Signals and Div. R.A. will submit their requirements to A.D.A.S. who will allot them the necessary back lines in the buries.

(b) Instead of Signal Manual Code Calls being used after Zero (Sec I-5-(b) the special calls issued by the Fifth Army and circulated under separate cover will be used.

(2) Telephone system. Field Cable.

It must be impressed upon all ranks that the supply of cable is very limited and unnecessary waste must be avoided.
Units must not use their mobile equipment except in emergency, and the fact that it has been used should be reported at once.
Metallic circuits only are to be laid.
If an earthed circuit has to be employed fullerphone must be used.

(3) Visual.

German visual stations are reported at D.8.c.65.57, D.20.a.65.80., E.20.c.30.40., D.25.c.50.62., D.12.a.45.00 (Sheet 28 N.E.) These points are almost certain to make good O.P's and Brigades should attempt to use them in their communications.

(4) PIGEONS.

During operations "PRACTICE" messages must not be sent, even when birds have to be released without operation messages.

(5) AEROPLANES.

Troops will signal to aeroplanes by flares and "WATSON" FANS (latter if procurable) and by Ground Panels from Battalion and Brigade H.Q.
Aeroplanes will signal by lamps, KLAXON HORNS and Very Lights.

(6) TANKS.

Tanks signal to Infantry by means of red, green and white discs (No. 2 Edition of Tank Signals will be used).
Infantry may signal to tanks by making use of the Signal Tank, one of which will operate on each Divisional front. These are easily recognised by being of the old pattern without guns but carrying a wireless mast on the roof.

(7) LATERAL COMMUNICATIONS.

When in the line units must establish communication with units on either flank, either by telephone, visual or runner. Bde. H.Q. must be linked up laterally by Bde. Signals at the first opportunity.

(8) Captured Signalling Equipment.

All captured signalling equipment must be handed over without delay to the Div. Ordnance Officer (through Div. Signals) who will issue to the Officer i/c Signals of the Division any serviceable telephones or telephone equipment which is required to replace deficiencies.

(9) Two message dogs have been allotted to the 55th Division. All ranks should be warned that dogs carrying message pouches on their collars are not to be detained, except for the purpose of having the message read by an officer.

(10) ROCKETS.

An issue of message carrying rockets is being made. This rocket carrier has a range of 1200 yards, whistles during its flight and burns a magnesium glare. It is very accurate in direction and fairly accurate in range. Each Company H.Q. will carry a proportion of these rockets. 6 rockets and one firing tube could be carried by one man, the whole bundle weighing about 20 lbs. It should not be fired too close to a Hd. Qrs. The Bde. Signal Officer will issue instructions for firing them.

(ii) MISCALLANEOUS.

A Forward Signal Station should be clearly and properly marked so that it may not be "mopped up" in case the signal party has pushed on ahead of the moppers up.

Operators and linemen must be instructed not to call up continuously on lines that are apparently down. The lines may perhaps be earthed and this calling will jam the Power Buzzer. Calls must be made for a short time only, say one minute in every four.

As the enemy will be falling back on positions more or less prepared the ordinary precautions of trench warfare against overhearing must be enforced at the earliest possible moment.

It is again impressed on all units that it is their duty to get in communication with the Brigade Forward Station with all possible speed and that they are responsible for the maintenance of that communication.

Captain,
Brigade Major, 49th Infantry Brigade.

25th July, 1917.

SECRET.

G.O.C.
2nd R. Irish Regt.
7th R. Innis Fus.
8th R. Innis Fus.
7/8th R. Irish Fus.
49th M.G. Company.
49th T.M. Battery.
157th Field Coy, R.E.
Staff Captain.
Bde. Intelligence Officer.
Bde. Signal Officer.
16th Div. (G).

49th Inf. Bde. No. S.O. 100/3 - 27-7-17.

Herewith Copy No ...**4**... of 49th INFANTRY BRIGADE INSTRUCTION FOR THE OFFENSIVE, INSTRUCTION No. 6, and APPENDIX "A", TIME TABLE OF ATTACK, to accompany INSTRUCTION No. 1.

Please acknowledge receipt.

[signature] Captain,
Brigade Major, 49th Infantry Brigade.

SECRET. Copy No ....

49TH INFANTRY BRIGADE INSTRUCTIONS FOR THE OFFENSIVE.

INSTRUCTION No. 6.

CONTACT AEROPLANES.

1. Two Contact Patrol aeroplanes, one to each of the two attacking Divisions, will be detailed by No. 21 Squadron, R.F.C.

2. These Contact Aeroplanes will be marked with a BLACK plaque projecting behind the right lower wing, thus

PLAQUE AS SEEN FROM BELOW.

3. In signalling to aeroplanes, infantry will follow the instructions laid down in S.S. 135, Appendix B., paras 4 and 5.

4. The following means will be used to show the most advanced position of the infantry :-

   (a) WHITE flares.

   (b) Watson Fans (if available).

5. Flares will be lit by Infantry in the front line

   (a) When called for by the Contact Patrol Aeroplanes by means of Klaxon horns and Very Lights. This call will, if the attack proceeds as arranged, only be made at times when the infantry are believed to have reached the BLUE, BLACK and GREEN LINES.

   (b) When the infantry consider it advisable to make known the position of their front line.

6. Dropping Stations for Divisional Headquarters will be as follows :-

15th Division	Will be notified later.
55th Division.	H.1.a.7.4.

27-7-17.

J.W.B.Will Captain,
Brigade Major, 49th Infantry Brigade.

SECRET.   Appendix "A".

TIME TABLE OF ATTACK.

To accompany 49TH INFANTRY BRIGADE INSTRUCTIONS FOR THE OFFENSIVE. (INSTRUCTION No. 1).

Serial No.	Time.	Action of Artillery.	Action of Infantry.
1.	00.00	Barrage put down on enemy front line	Infantry leave their trenches and advance to the assault.
2.	plus 00.06.	Barrage lifts off enemy front line and advances at rate of 100 yards in 4 minutes.	Infantry assault and capture enemy front system of trenches.
3.	plus 00.54R. 00.42C. 00.42L.	Protective barrage formed 300 yards in front of BLUE Line.	Infantry Halt and consolidate on BLUE Line.
4.	plus 01.15.	Barrage put down on whole front of attack.	Infantry assemble close under barrage in readiness to advance.
5.	plus 01.39 R. 01.23 C.& L.	Barrage lifts and advances at rate of 100 yards in 4 minutes.	Infantry advance and capture enemy second line system (STUTZPUNKT LINE)
6.	plus 02.07 R. 02.15 C. 01.59 L.	Protective barrage formed 300 yards in front of BLACK LINE.	Infantry halt and consolidate on BLACK LINE.
7.	plus 06.20	Barrage put down on whole Corps Front.	Infantry assemble close under barrage and prepare to advance.
8.	plus 06.28	Barrage lifts and advances at the rate of 100 yards in 4 minutes.	Infantry advance and capture the CHELUVELT -LANGEMARCK Line.
9.	plus 07.36 R. 07.28 C. 07.28 L.	Protective barrage formed 500 yards in front of GREEN Line.	Infantry Halt, and consolidate on GREEN LINE.
10.	plus 08.20	Protective barrage ceases on whole Corps front.	

R = On Right Corps Boundary.

C = On Divisional Boundary.

L = On Left Corps Boundary.

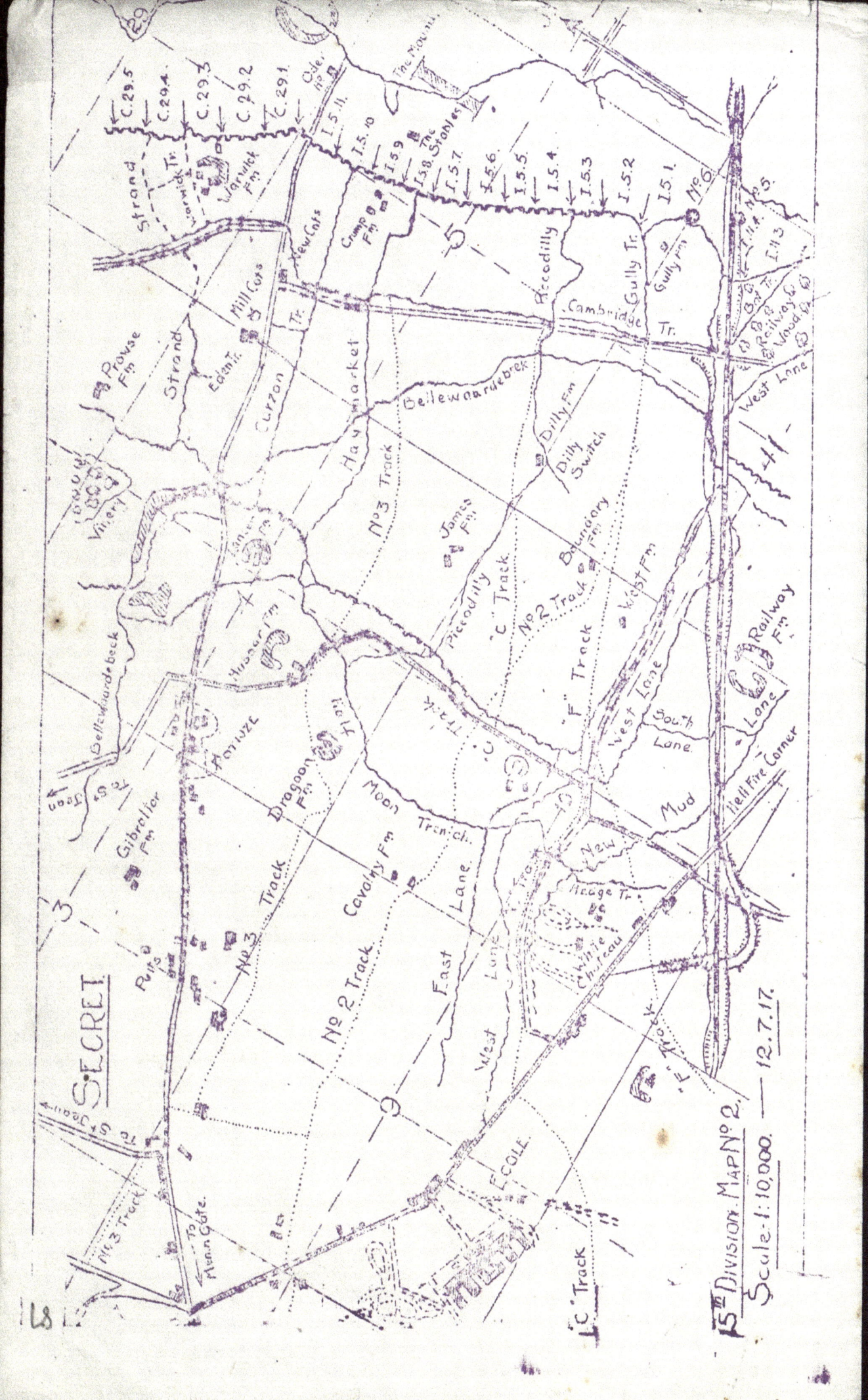

49th. I.B. No. S.C.C.2/119/1.

2nd. R.Irish Regt.
7th. R.Innis. Fus.
8th. R.Innis. Fus.
7/8th. R.Irish Fus.
49th. M.G.Coy.

Reference this office No. S.C.C.2/119 of Yesterday's ~~to-day's~~ date re issue of grenades, etc., these will be dumped at H.qrs. of units concerned in the WATOU Area and not in the BRANDHOEK Area ~~~~ on the 27th. inst.

H Bowen

Captain,
Staff Captain, 49th. Infantry Brigade.

2/c
25.7.17.

49th I.B. No. S.C.C. 2/119

2/R. Irish Regt.
7/R. Innis. Fus.
8/R. Innis. Fus.
7/8th R. Irish Fus.
49th M.G. Coy.

Issued in continuation of 49th I.B. Instructions for the Offensive - Instruction No.3.

The undermentioned Grenades etc., will be probably be dumped at respective Battalions and M.G. Coy. Headquarters in the BRANDHOEK-No.1. Area about 8 a.m. on the 27th inst.

Units will have to send parties forward to detonate and look after these grenades etc.

To each Battalion.

    1500 Mills No. 5 Grenades.
    1500 " No.23 Rifle Grenades.
    80 "P" Bombs.
    30 S.O.S. Rifle Grenades.
    4 boxes 1" V.L.
    4 " 1½" V.L.
    400 Ground flares.

To M.G. Coy.

    4 boxes 1" V.L.

Further details later.

          Captain.
          Staff Captain.
25.7.17.   49th Infantry Brigade.

NOTES ON THE COUNTRY NORTH-EAST OF THE ZONNEBEKE-STADEN

LINE TO THE BRUGES - GHENT CANAL.

(a) ZONNEBEKE - STADEN LINE TO A

LINE ROULERS - HOOGLEDE.

TOPOGRAPHY.
The ZONNEBEKE - STADEN line is constructed along the PASSCHENDAELE Ridge - a northern extension of the WYTSCHAETE - MESSINES Ridge. This ridge, on which are situated the villages of WESTROOSEBEKE, PASSCHENDAELE, BROODSEINDE and BERCELAERE, runs due north and south at an angle to the present Army front.

From its northern extremity the HOOGLEDE Spur extends eastward, and commands the low lying country round ROULERS.

From PASSCHENDAELE, a spur extends south-east bearing on its highest point the village of MOORSLEDE. This spur subsequently throws out three spurs south of ROULERS, the most northern of these runs almost to the outskirts of ROULERS at ZUIDMOLEN, the centre spur runs to DUIZENDZUINEN and the southern to DADIZEELE.

For an army advancing in a north-easterly direction these three spurs would provide a flank position of some depth against attack from the south and south-east.

From the WESTROOSBEKE - PASSCHENDAELE road there is good observation to the east where the country is flat and for the most part not enclosed.

The MOORSLEDE - DADIZEELE ridge overlooks the country to the east, but observation is much more limited than would be expected from a study of the map. From BERCELAERE a good view is obtained to the east and south-east.

Between the PASSCHENDAELE ridge and ROULERS the country, which is cultivated, is practicable for cavalry and infantry except in the valley of the MANDEL which enters ROULERS from the west. Here the fields are small and are enclosed with wire. Artillery could not as a rule move far from the roads.

ROULERS before the war was an important manufacturing town of some 25,000 inhabitants, lying partly on a lower level than that of the surrounding country.

Southward and eastward from ROULERS the country slopes away into the valley of the LYS.

(b) FROM A LINE ROULERS - HOOGLEDE

TO THE BRUGES - GHENT CANAL.

To the north and northeast of the line HOOGLEDE - ROULERS there is no important change in the elevation of the country until the line THIELT - THOUROUT - WIJNENDAELE is reached. There are three points on this general line which afford exceptionally good observation north and south :-
    (a) the small ridge on which THIELT stands.
    (b) the ridge north of COOLSCAMP.
    (c) the ridge north of THOUROUT on the edge of which is the WIJEN - DAELE Chateau.

The last named is of particular importance as it provides observation over the flat country south of the PASSCHENDAELE Canal, which is also overlooked from the fortified positions on the dunes now held by the enemy.

The.

- 2 -

      The country is, on the whole, open on the lower ground, but on the higher ground, in the THIELT - LICHTERVEKDE - THOUROUT area, there are a considerable number of hedges. These are for the most part small, but many are planted with linns of trees which limit the field of view.

      A continuous belt of pine forest runs east and west from THOUROUT to ECLOO, this area is easily passable by all arms as the forest is divided into small regular lots by roads and tracks.

ROADS.   It is reported that the main roads running north-east have been kept in good condition. These consist mainly of "pavé" though there are some good macadam roads. The side roads are probably in bad repair.

Fifth Army "I".
15th July, 1917.

(sd) A. JOHN HUGH CRAIK, Lt.
    for Lieut-Colonel,
      General Staff.

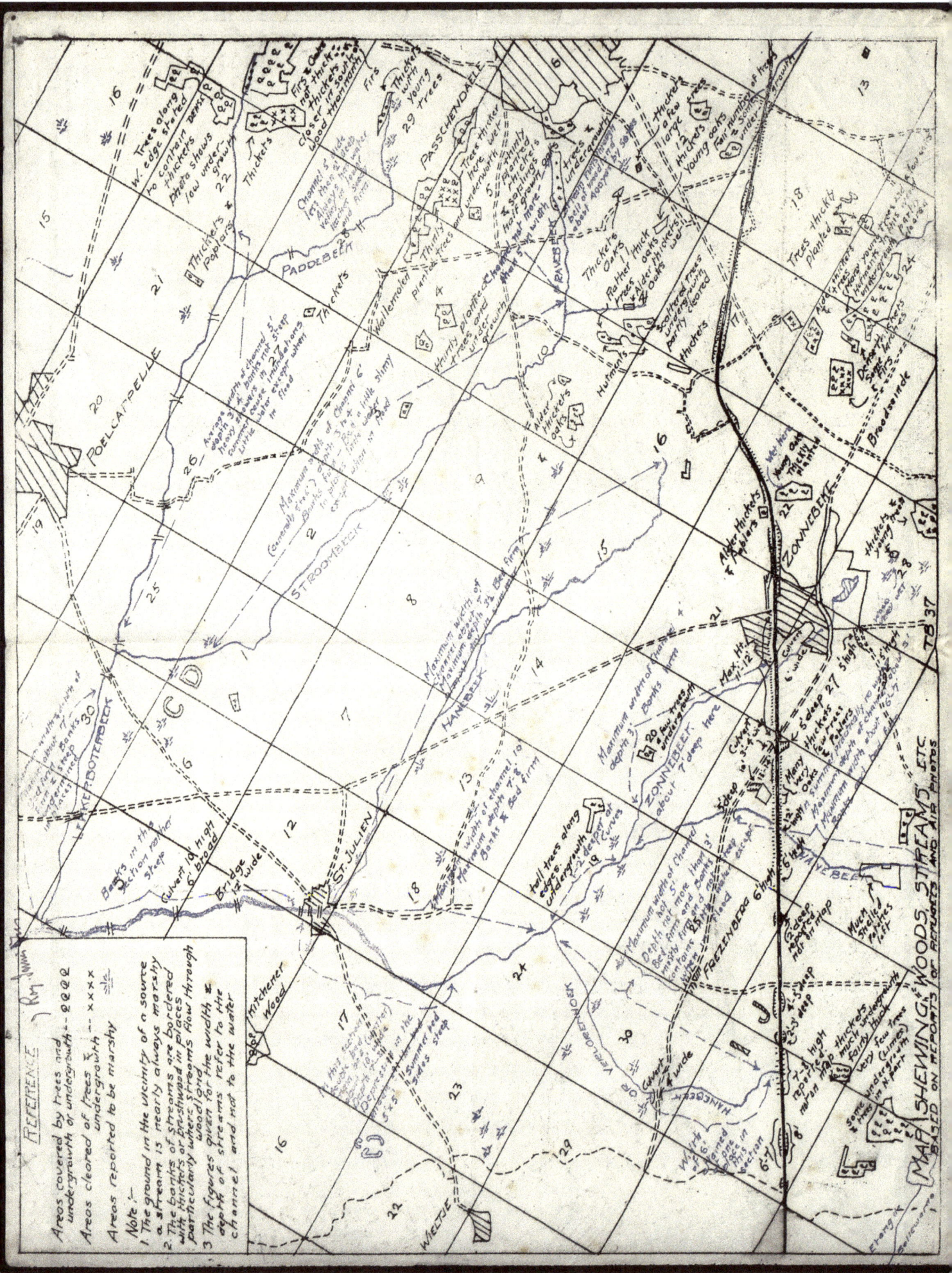

RAID

SECRET

By **49ᵀᴴ INFANTRY BRIGADE.**

ON ENEMY TRENCHES

BETWEEN

MAEDELSTEDE & PECKHAM.

H.Q. 16th Division (G)
G.O.C. 16th Div.Arty
2nd R. Irish Regt
7th R. Innis Fus.
8th R. Innis Fus.
7/8th R. Irish Fus.
49th M.G. Company,
49th T. M. B.
O.C. Centre Group.

S E C R E T.

49th Infy Bde No. B.O.89/2 - 12-1-17.

Reference my B.O.89 of 11-1-17.

ZERO HOUR will be 9.30 p.m.

ACKNOWLEDGE.

Captain,

a/Brigade Major, 49th Infantry Brigade.

S E C R E T. Copy No........

49th Infantry Brigade Order No. 89 - 10-1-17.

Raid by 49th Infantry Brigade on Enemy Trenches between
HAEDELSTEDE FARM AND PECKHAM.

Ref. Map 28.S.W.2.
    Scale 1/10000 Edn. 3.E.

1.   A Raid will be made on 12th January, 1917.

   Area of raid will be from enemy's front trench between
N.24.c.35.55 and N.30.a.68.96 to a depth of approximately
250 yards, N.24.d.27.55 to N.30.b.28.97

   Time Table is attached (Appendix 9).

   ZERO HOUR to be notified later.

2.   The object is - to penetrate enemy's support line and
ascertain the condition of those trenches, to capture
prisoners, Machine Guns, Trench Mortars and destroy
emplacements, dugouts, etc.

3.   Detail of Troops and Trench Mortars to be used.

      O.C. Raid.......Lieut. Colonel K.C. WELDON, D.S.O.

         2 Coys....7/8th R. Irish Fus.
         3 Stokes Guns.
         2 2" Trench Mortars.

      Covered by 16th Divisional Artillery (WYTSCHAETE Group)
      and IXth Corps H.A.

4.   At ZERO minus 2 hours a Feint will be made on enemy's front
line between N.30.a.42.40 and N.30.a.12.04.

   Detail of Troops and Trench Mortars to be used :-

      O.C. Enterprise........Captain V.H. Parr, M.C.

         20 Other Ranks.
         8 Stokes Guns.
         4 2" Trench Mortars.
      Covered by 16th Divisional Artillery.

5.   O.C. 8th R. Innis Fus will clear his trenches North of
PALL MALL as required by O.C. Enterprise.

6.   Care will be taken by O.C. Raid and O.C. Enterprise that all
prisoners, also papers taken from them and enemy dead are sent
to Brigade Headquarters immediately.

7.   Watches will be synchronised at minus 6 hours, and again
at minus 3 hours.

8.   Attached are the following copies of Orders and
Arrangements made, also Maps :-

1. Preliminary Orders   Appendix I

2. Scheme for Raid by O.C.7/8th R. Irish   Appendix II
    Fus.

3. Orders for Raid by O.C.7/8th R.Irish Fus.   Appendix III.

4. Orders for Enterprise by O.C. 7th   Appendix IV.
    R. Innis Fus.

5. Orders by G.O.C. 16th Div. Artillery   Appendix V.

6. Arrangements by O.C. 49th T.M.Group.   Appendix VI.

7. Arrangements by O.C. 49th M.G. Coy.   Appendix VII.

8. Signal Communication.   Appendix VIII

9. Time Table.   Appendix IX.

10. Map A. Showing Raid Area and Barrage

11 Map B.(1) and (2). Showing Area of Enterprise and
                        Barrages.

                                    B. Bawley
                                        Captain,

                    a/Brigade Major, 49th Infantry Brigade.

Appendix I.

S E C R E T.

PRELIMINARY ORDERS FOR RAID.

A Raid will be carried out on the 12th instant.

FORCE TO BE EMPLOYED.

    O.C. Raid............Lieut.Col. K.C. Weldon, D.S.O.

    Two Companies......7/8th R. Irish Fus.
    4 2" Trench Mortars.
    8 Stokes Mortars.
    Covered by 16th Divisional Artillery.

OBJECT.

    To penetrate to enemy's support line, ascertaining the state of these trenches, capture machine guns, trench mortars and prisoners.

AREA TO BE RAIDED.

    Enemy front line trench between N.24.c.85.55 and N.30.a.68.96 to a depth of approximately 250 yards, N.24.d.27.55 to N.30.b.28.97.

PREPARATION.

    Wire will be cut by 2" T.M's along the whole Brigade Front daily. Stokes will assist by scattering wire that has already been torn up by 2" T.M's.
    4.5" Howitzers will assist by cutting on raid front, and also between N.30.a.42.40 and N.30.a.12.04.
    All gaps will be kept open by 18-pdrs, Stokes Guns and Lewis Guns.
    It is essential that as much attention be paid to the various points on Brigade Front as to the area to be raided.
    Concentrated bombardments will take place at various points, (two on Raid Front), to clear away the enemy's wire.

METHOD.

    There will be no Artillery Bombardment on Raid Front immediately preceeding Raid.
Point. At ZERO minus 10 minutes an intense bombardment with Artillery, Stokes and 2" T.M's will take place on enemy's front line and communication trenches between N.30.a.42.40 and N.30.a.12.04. At ZERO barrage will lift to support trenches, and keep up a slow rate of fire until ZERO plus 5 minutes.
Raiding Party. The raiding party will be drawn up in front of their wire before ZERO, ready to move forward. At ZERO party will move forward and enter trenches. At ZERO plus 5 minutes, Artillery will open a Box Barrage round the area to be raided. Heavy Artillery will fire on suspected machine guns, etc.
    Party will remain in 30 minutes. Artillery not to cease until parties are all reported back.

Appendix I (Contd)

VICKERS GUNS.

O.C. 49th M.G. Company will arrange for indirect fire on all Communication Trenches, Roads, Tracks, etc, in rear of and leading to area of raid.

TRENCH MORTARS.

O.C. 49th Trench Mortar Group will arrange for a proportion of his guns to fire during bombardment at ZERO minus 10 minutes, and a proportion on enemy's front line and communication trenches either flank of Raid Area at ZERO plus 5 minutes.

L M Morley
Captain,
a/Brigade Major, 49th Infantry Brigade.

Issued through Signals.

Copy No. 1 to 16th Division.
" " 2   16th Div. Artillery.
" " 3   O.C. Centre Group.
" " 4   2nd R. Irish Regt.
" " 5   7th R. Innis Fus.
" " 6   8th R. Innis Fus.
" " 7   7/8th R. Irish Fus.
" " 8   49th M.G. Company.
" " 9   49th T.M. Group.
" " 10-11 War Diary.
" " 12 File.

Appendix I (Contd)

16th Division.
16th Div Artillery.
O.C. Centre Group.
2nd R. Irish Regt.
7th R. Innis Fus.
8th R. Innis Fus.
7/8th R. Irish Fus.
49th T. M. Battery.
49th M.G. Company.
Staff Captain.

SECRET.

49th Infy Bde No. S.O.945/1 - 6-1-17.

Reference this Office No. S.O.945 of 3-1-17, (PRELIMINARY ORDERS FOR RAID).

It has now been decided to send in a small party at the point where the feint is directed (Between N.30.a.42.40 and N.30.a.12.04).

O.C. 7th R. Innis Fus will arrange for a party of not more than 20 (all ranks) to enter the enemy trenches between above points, as soon as the barrage lifts.

They will remain in enemy's trenches not more than 5 minutes. Their sole object will be to obtain identifications, if possible prisoners, and make a note of the state of enemy's front line. They will not go beyond enemy's front line trench.

When Barrage lifts at ZERO, it should creep back to the standing barrage. The Box Barrage will be continued for 10 minutes.

O.C. 7th R. Innis Fus. will take his party out of the line at once, and send them back to LOCRE to train. They will be billetted at Brigade School under arrangements to be made by Staff Captain.

L. R. Bowley
Captain,
a/Brigade Major, 49th Infantry Brigade.

Appendix I (Contd)

16th Div Artillery.
O.C. Centre Group.
7th R. Innis Fus.
7/8th R. Irish Fus.
16th Division.   )
2nd R. Irish Regt.)
8th R. Innis Fus.) For
49th T.M. Battery.) Information.
49th M.G. Company.)
Staff Captain.   )

SECRET.

49th Infy Bde No. S.O.945/2 - 8-1-17.

Reference this Office No. S.O.945 of 3-1-17, and S.O.945/2 of 6-1-17.

The Feint on enemy's front trench between N.30.a.42.40 and N.30.a.12.04 will now take place at - 2 Hours.

All details remain the same.

The first four units as mentioned above will please acknowledge receipt.

Captain,
a/Brigade Major, 49th Infantry Brigade.

O.C. "A" Coy.,
 "   "B" "
 "   "C" "
 "   "D" "
2/Lt. W.D. Porter,

8th R. Innis. Fus. No. S/217/1 - 12/1/17.

SECRET.

Ref. Map 28.S.W.?, Scale 1/10000.
Edition 3 E.

RAID BY 7/8th R. IRISH FUSILIERS.

Further to this Office No. S/217 of 10th inst..

Zero will be about 9.15 p.m. - exact time will be notified later.

1. **1st.** A <u>Feint Raid</u> by small party of 7th R. Innis. Fus will be carried out at Zero minus 2 hours. This party will enter enemy trenches at about N.30.a.08.03.
O.C. Feint Raid will be at Left Coy. H.Q..
O's.C. "A" & "D" Coys., will arrange to clear the front line for 4 or 5 bays North of PALL MALL (old) moving the men from these bays further N. & S. respectively, in order to leave a clear trench for the raiding party, who will have a support of 10 men remaining in the trench.
Trench will be cleared by Zero minus 3 hours.
When the feint raid is over, our men will at once be moved back to their previous dispositions.

2. **SIGNALS.**
The signal to return from enemy lines will be 3 green Very Lights.
Watches will be synchronised at Zero minus 6 and minus 3 hours.
The Signal Officer will arrange that all lines are left clear for use of O.C. Feint Raid & O.C. 7th R. Innis. Fus. - latter will be at FORT VICTORIA.

3. **LEWIS GUNS.**
O's.C. "A" & "D" Coys., will arrange for covering fire on flanks from N.30.a.30.40 to N.30.a.45.35, and from N.30.c.05.95 to N.30.c.07.70. Particular attention must be paid to the salient at N.30.a.30.25 from which an enemy M.G. is known to fire.

4. **ACKNOWLEDGE.**

W.E.N. Arm
Capt.,
Adjutant. 8th R. Innis. Fusrs..

Secret.   80th R. In.   S/217/1/d/—
          Raid by 7/8 R.I.F.   12th Jan 1917
                              Refce MAP. 28 S.W.2 Edit. 3E
Further to this office S/217 of 10th inst.   Scale 1/10.000.
    Zero will be about 9.15 pm, — exact time will be
    notified later.
1. A Feint Raid by small party of 7th R. Innis Fus (at Zero – 2 hours) will be carried out.
   This party will enter enemy trenches at about ~~N 30~~

O.C. Feint Raid will > N. 30 a 08.03.
be at Left Coy. Hq.   ~~O.C. 'A' Coy will arrange~~
   Os.C A + D Coys will arrange to clear the front line for
   4 or 5 bays North of PALL MALL (old) ~~or~~ moving
   ~~the~~ the men from these bays further N. and S
   respectively, in order to leave a clear trench
   for the raiding party, who will have a support
   of 10 men remaining in the trench.
   ~~Trench will be cleared~~ by ZERO – 3 hours.
   When the feint raid is over, our men will at once
   be moved back to their previous dispositions.
2. Signals.
   The signal to return from enemy lines will be
     3 Green Very Lights.
   Watches will be synchronised at Zero – 6, & – 3 hours.
     The Signals Officer will arrange that all lines
   are left clear for use of O.C. ~~Raid~~ Feint Raid, & OC.
   7th R. Innis Fus., — the latter will be at FORT VICTORIA
3. LEWIS GUNS.
     Os.C. A + D Coys will arrange for covering fire on flanks
   from N 30 a 3.10 to N 30 a 45.35, and from N 30 c 05.35
   to N 30 c 07.70. Particular attention must
   be paid to the small salient at N 30 a 30.25 from
   enemy ~~where~~ an M.G. is ~~safe~~ known to fire. which point
4. Acknowledge.

SECRET.

PRELIMINARY ORDERS FOR RAID.

A Raid will be carried out on the 12th instant.

FORCE TO BE EMPLOYED.

    O.C. Raid.............Lieut.Col. K.C. Weldon, D.S.O.

    Two Companies......7/8th R. Irish Fus.
    4 2" Trench Mortars.
    8 Stokes Mortars.
    Covered by 16th Divisional Artillery.

OBJECT.

    To penetrate to enemy's support line, ascertaining the state of these trenches, capture machine guns, trench mortars and prisoners.

AREA TO BE RAIDED.

    Enemy front line trench between N.24.c.85.55 and N.30.a.68.96 to a depth of approximately 250 yards, N.24.d.27.55 to N.30.b.28.97.

PREPARATION.

    Wire will be cut by 2" T.M's along the whole Brigade Front daily. Stokes will assist by scattering wire that has already been torn up by 2" T.M's.
    4.5" Howitzers will assist by cutting on raid front, and also between N.30.a.42.40 and N.30.a.12.04.
    All gaps will be kept open by 18-pdrs, Stokes Guns and Lewis Guns.
    It is essential that as much attention be paid to the various points on Brigade Front as to the area to be raided.
    Concentrated bombardments will take place at various points, (two on Raid Front), to clear away the enemy's wire.

METHOD.

    There will be no Artillery Bombardment on Raid Front immediately preceeding Raid.
Feint. At ZERO minus 10 minutes an intense bombardment with Artillery, Stokes and 2" T.M's will take place on enemy's front line and communication trenches between N.30.a.42.40 and N.30.a.12.04. At ZERO barrage will lift to support trenches, and keep up a slow rate of fire until ZERO plus 5 minutes.
Raiding Party. The raiding party will be drawn up in front of their wire before ZERO, ready to move forward. At ZERO party will move forward and enter trenches. At ZERO plus 5 minutes, Artillery will open a Box Barrage round the area to be raided. Heavy Artillery will fire on suspected machine guns, etc.
    Party will remain in 30 minutes. Artillery not to cease until parties are all reported back.

VICKERS GUNS.

O.C. 49th M. G. Company will arrange for indirect fire on all Communication Trenches, Roads, Tracks, etc, in rear of and leading to area of raid.

TRENCH MORTARS.

O.C. 49th Trench Mortar Group will arrange for a proportion of his guns to fire during bombardment at ZERO minus 10 minutes, and a proportion on enemy's front line and communication trenches either flank of Raid Area at ZERO plus 5 minutes.

[signature]
Captain,

a/Brigade Major, 49th Infantry Brigade.

Issued through Signals.

Copy No. 1 to 16th Division.
" 2 16th Div. Artillery.
" 3 O.C. Contre Group.
" 4 2nd R. Irish Regt.
" 5 7th R. Innis Fus.
" 6 8th R. Innis Fus.
" 7 7/8th R. Irish Fus.
" 8 49th M.G. Company.
" 9 49th T.M. Group.
" 10-11 War Diary.
" 12 File.

16th Division.
16th Div Artillery.
O.C. Centre Group.
2nd R. Irish Regt.
7th R. Innis Fus.
8th R. Innis Fus.
7/8th R. Irish Fus.
49th T. M. Battery,
49th M.G. Company.
Staff Captain.

SECRET.

49th Infy Bde No. S.O.945/1 - 6-1-17.

Reference this Office No. S.O.945 of 3-1-17, (PRELIMINARY ORDERS FOR RAID).

It has now been decided to send in a small party at the point where the feint is directed (Between N.30.a.42.40 and N.30.a.12.04).

O.C. 7th R. Innis Fus will arrange for a party of not more than 20 (all ranks) to enter the enemy trenches between above points, as soon as the barrage lifts.

They will remain in enemy's trenches not more than 5 minutes. Their sole object will be to obtain identifications, if possible, prisoners, and make a note of the state of enemy's front line. They will not go beyond enemy's front line trench.

When Barrage lifts at ZERO, it should creep back to the standing barrage. The Box Barrage will be continued for 10 minutes.

O.C. 7th R. Innis Fus. will take his party out of the line at once, and send them back to LOCRE to train. They will be billetted at Brigade School under arrangements to be made by Staff Captain.

Captain,
a/Brigade Major, 49th Infantry Brigade.

16th Div Artillery.
O.C. Centre Group.
7th R. Innis Fus.
7/8th R. Irish Fus.
16th Division.   )
2nd R. Irish Regt.   )
8th R. Innis Fus.   ) For
49th T.M. Battery.   ) Information.
49th M.G. Company.   )
Staff Captain.   )

SECRET.

49th Infy Bde No. S.O.945/2 - 8-1-17.

    Reference this Office No. S.O.945 of 3-1-17, and S.O.945/2 of 6-1-17.

    The Feint on enemy's front trench between N.30.a.42.40 and N.30.a.12.04 will now take place at - 2 Hours.

    All details remain the same.

    The first four units as mentioned above will please acknowledge receipt.

Captain,

a/Brigade Major, 49th Infantry Brigade.

H.Q. 16th Division (G).
G.O.C. 16th Div. Arty.
2nd R. Irish Regt.
7th R. Innis Fus.
8th R. Innis Fus.
7/8th R. Irish Fus.
O.C. Centre Group.
49th M.G. Company.
49th T. M. B.

S E C R E T.

49th Infy Bde No. B.O.89 - 11-1-17.

Herewith Orders and Arrangements made for Raid on January 12th, 1917.

A few minor alterations were made at a Conference held this morning and are known to all concerned.

ZERO HOUR will be about 9.15 p.m. Exact time to be notified later.

ACKNOWLEDGE. √

Captain,

a/Brigade Major, 49th Infantry Brigade.

S E C R E T.   Appendix II.

SCHEME FOR BATTALION RAID BY 7/8TH ROYAL IRISH FUSILIERS.

1 GENERAL IDEA.

To raid enemy's front and support line trenches between lines running East and West, through N.24.c.9.5 and N.30.a.7.9 to a depth of 200 yards with the object of securing prisoners, and trophies and doing all possible damage to M.G. and T.M. Emplacements, etc, and looking for Gas Cylinders, and if found bring one back if possible.

2 DATE ....

  Hour................

3. STRENGTH OF PARTY.

Two Companies divided into four parties, each under one officer, the latter parties being sub-divided into bombing squads.

4. TIME.

Time taken. Five minutes to cross.
Maximum time allowed in trenches - thirty minutes.

5. RETURN.

All parties on returning must immediately report their arrival to O.C. Enterprise at Coy H.Q. in VIA GELLIA.

6. DISTINGUISHING MARKS.

Faces and hands will be blackened and countersign will be made known to everyone prior to raid.

7. DRESS AND EQUIPMENT.

All officers will carry torches and revolvers and bayonet men will carry torches fixed on their rifles. All bombers will carry eight bombs and shillelaghs, and all carriers will carry at least twelve bombs in a bucket and be armed with shillelaghs. Two pairs wire cutters per squad will be carried in addition to those attached to men's rifles and all N.C.Os and men will wear sidearms.

8. FLAGMEN. The flagmen of each of the four parties will leave white flags at the points where they cut through our wire.
9. WATCHES. Watches will be synchronised FOUR hours before ZERO time at Coy H.Q. in VIA GELLIA, and checked again TWO hours before ZERO.

10. COMMUNICATIONS

O.C. Enterprise, Lieut. Col K.C. WELDON, will be at new Coy H.Q. in VIA GELLIA which will be in direct communication with the Artillery, Brigade H.Q. and the two Companies in the HUN Line.

11. ACTION OF ARTILLERY.

To form a box barrage round the area to be raided, marked RED on the attached map: not to commence firing till the raiding party is in (i.e. plus five minutes) and not to stop firing till the return of the raiding party.

12. ACTION OF T.MS AND L.GS.

All Medium T.M's, Stokes Guns and Vickers to fire on Communication Trenches leading to the area selected for raiding in, (marked on attached map).

Appendix II (Contd)

13. FORWARD AID POST.

The M.O. will arrange to form a forward Regtl. Aid Post at Head of KETCHEN AVENUE, in addition to his post near BEAVER HAT.

14. ACTION OF INFANTRY.

At minus 5 (five minutes) the four parties of infantry must be through their own wire ready formed up to move forward at ZERO.

15. SIGNAL FOR WITHDRAWAL.

"Golden Rain Rocket" fired from our front line top of VIA GELLIA.

(sd) K.O. WELDON, Lieut. Colonel,

Commanding 7/8th R. Irish Fusiliers.

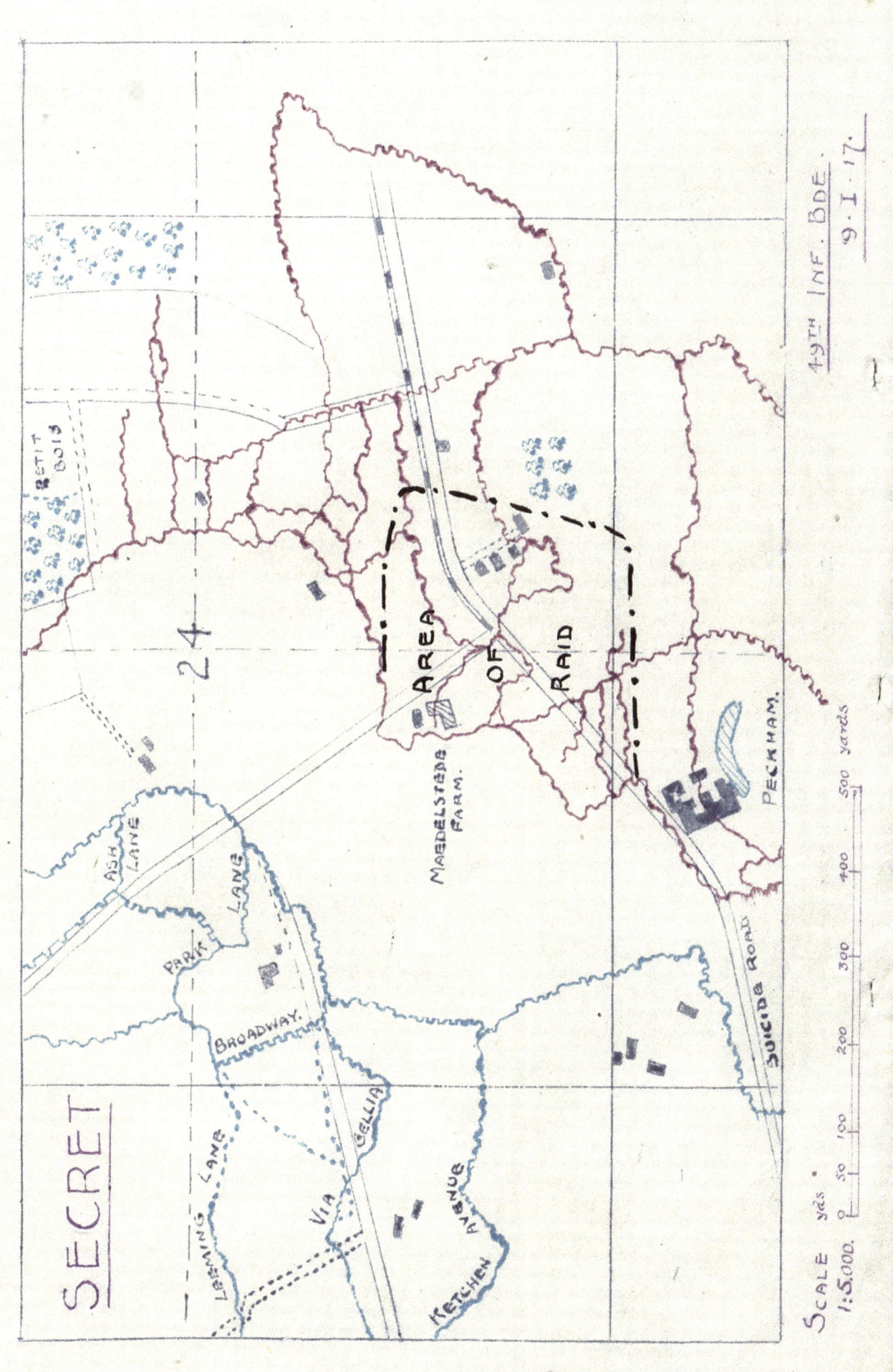

SECRET.

Appendix III.

ORDERS FOR RAID BY LIEUT. COLONEL. K.C. WELDON, D.S.O, Commanding,
7/8TH ROYAL IRISH FUSILIERS.

****

Reference Map attached.

DATE................

HOUR................

STRENGTH OF PARTIES.

Four parties as detailed below will raid the enemy's trenches between N.24.c.85.55 and N.30.a.68.96 to a depth of approximately 250 yards N.24.d.27.55 to N.30.b.28.97, all parties moving forward to the attack at ZERO.

No. 1 Party under 2/Lieut A.C. YOUNG........"C" Company.
No. 2 Party under 2/Lieut J.D. BAKER........"B" Company.
No. 3 Party under 2/Lieut E.J. MACMILLAN..."D" Company.
No. 4 Party under 2/Lieut T. GERATY........"D" Company.

Nos 1 and 2 Parties under Capt N.P. KNOWLES with Coy Signallers will pass through our wire in Valley at N.24.c.3.1 and be ready formed up outside it at minus 5 (five) minutes.

Objective No. 1 Party.....A. See attached Map.
Objective No. 2 Party.....B. See attached Map.

Nos 3 and 4 Parties 2/Lieut E.S. BIRD with Coy Signallers will pass through our wire where PARK LANE joins the Firing Line and be ready formed up outside our wire at minus 5 minutes.

Objective No. 3 Party...C. See attached Map.
Objective No. 4 Party...D. See attached Map.

SUPERVISION OF PARTIES.

Nos 1, 2, 3 and 4 Parties will each consist of the following :-
1.(One) Officer.
1.(One) Senior N.C.O.
2.(Two) Stretcher Bearers.
2.(Two) Flagmen.
6.(Six) Bombing squads of one N.C.O and six men, (1.c, 2 Bayonet Men, two bombers, two carriers)

GUIDING TAPE.

The rear squad of Nos 1 and 4 Parties will lay a tracing tape from the points of exit from our line to point of entry in Enemy's line, both ends of which will be firmly secured.

COUNTERSIGN.   "WATERLOO".

COMMUNICATIONS.

The Battalion Signalling Officer will arrange for one line to communicate with officer in charge Nos. 1 and 2 Parties from head of VIA GELLIA, and one line to communicate with officer in charge Nos. 3 and 4 parties from bomb-proof dugout in front line N. of GLORY HOLE.

Appendix III (Contd)

In the event of these wires being cut resort will be had to communication with special Signalling Lamp, the following Code will be employed in either case :-

    1. Have entered enemy's trenches.
    2. Bombs required.
    3. Prisoners taken.
    4. Raiders returning.

GAPS IN OUR WIRE.

O.C. "C" Coy will be responsible that two gaps are cut in our wire as soon as it is dark on the night of........ at the following points, and white flags placed in them to mark them.-
By the flagmen of No 1 Party at N.24.c.3.1.
By the flagmen of No. 2 Party opposite where the Southern entrance to VIA GELLIA joins the firing line.

O.C. "D" Coy will be responsible that two gaps are cut as soon as it is dark on the night of.........at the following points, and white flags placed in them to mark them.
By the flagmen of No. 3 Party fifty yards N. of BROADWAY.
By the flagmen of No. 4 Party where PARK LANE joins firing line.
All flagmen will be stationed at these gaps with megaphones to assist them in directing our men back into our trenches on their return.

IDENTIFICATION.

It must be impressed on all ranks that it is most important to secure identification in the form of prisoners, portions of uniform, or papers taken from the bodies of any of the enemy who may have been killed. Every man should carry his jack-knife for the purpose of cutting off shoulder straps, etc.

MEDICAL ARRANGEMENTS.

Special instructions have been issued direct to Coys for evacuation of wounded.

POLICE.

O.C. "A" Coy will arrange to police VIA GELLIA from Zero until all wounded have been evacuated from Dressing Station in VIA GELLIA. On no account are men to be allowed to loiter round the Dressing Station.

PRISONERS.

All prisoners will be sent in first instance to officers in charge of "C" and "D" Coys Raiding Parties who will retain them, bring them back with their parties when returning, and will hand them over to the Regtl. Police at Battalion H.Q. in VIA GELLIA.

                (sd) K.C. WELDON, Lieut .Colonel,
      Commanding 7/8th R. Irish Fus.

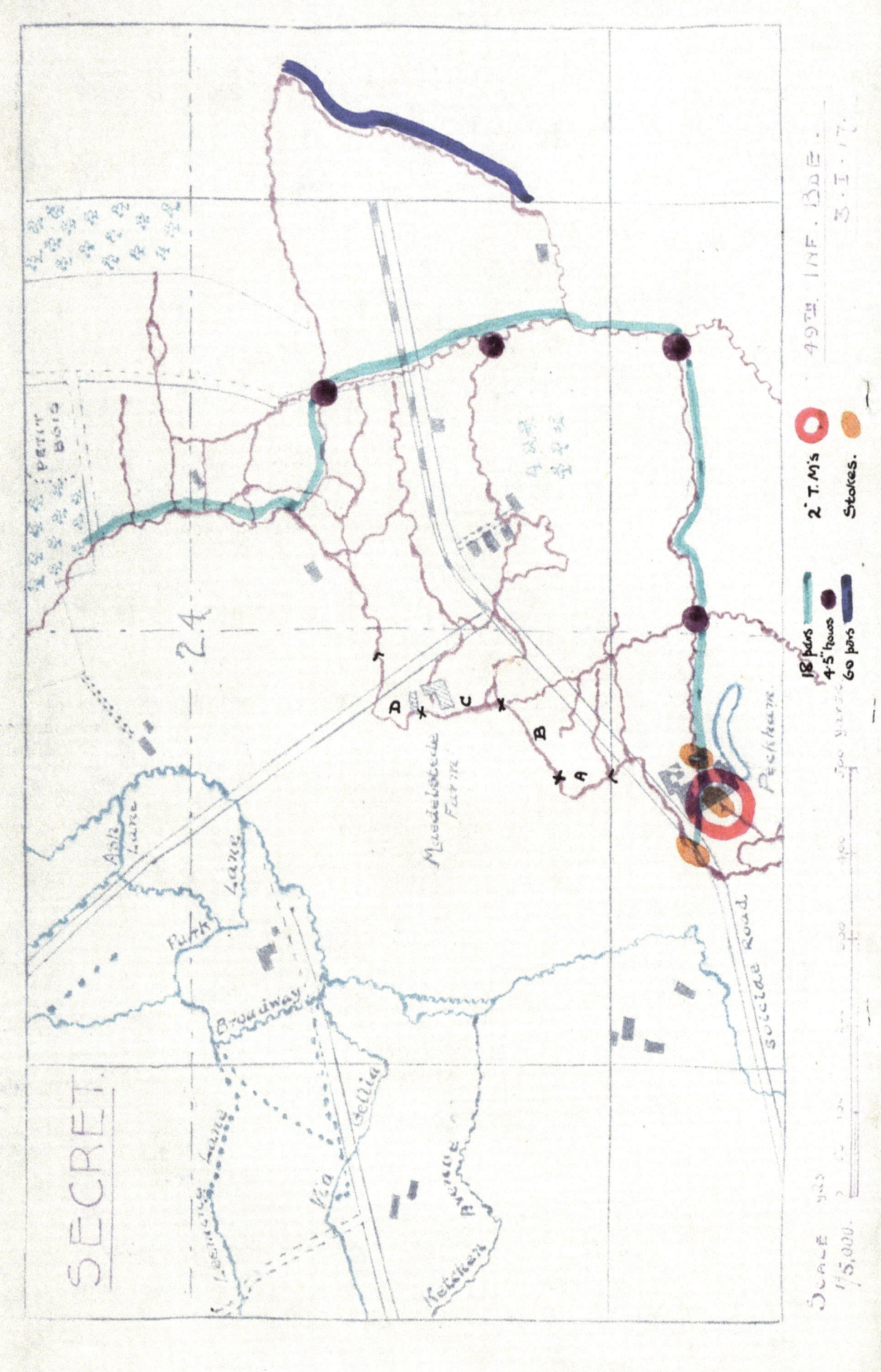

Appendix IV.

S E C R E T.   Copy No. 1.

ORDERS FOR DUMMY RAID BY O.C. 7TH R. INNISKILLING FUS.
===

1. **GENERAL.** A small raid will be carried out by the 7th R. Innis Fus as a feint to the raid of the 7/8th R. Irish Fus on the night of the 12th instant on the German front line between the points N.30.a.42.40 and N.30.a.12.04.

2. **OBJECT.** The object of the raid will be to obtain information, identifications, if possible prisoners, and make a note of the state of the enemy's front line.

3. **STRENGTH.**   O.C. Raid Party..........Captain V.H.Parr.

    The strength of the raiding party will be -

    1 Officer and 20 Other Ranks.

    Support 1 N.C.O and 10 men with 4 stretcher bearers,
    (Emergency)   (to remain in our trenches)

4. **DESCRIPTION OF GROUND.** The contour of the ground forms a re-entrant falling towards the West from the ridge running North and South through N.30.a.0.0. The German line runs generally N.W. from near the above reference. On the left of the Battalion frontage N.29.4 a row of pollarded willows runs S.S.W. one third of the way across No Man's Land towards the German line. Between this row of trees and the crest of the ridge is the spot chosen for the raid, entering the German line at a gap in the enemy wire about the centre of the bay shown in their front line on aerial photograph.

5. **ARTILLERY ACTION.** At Zero minus 2 hours an intense bombardment with artillery, Stokes and 2" T.M's will take place on enemy's front line and communication trenches between N.30.a.42.40 and N.30.a.12.04. At Zero minus 1hr.50 mins. barrage will creep back to enemy's support line, and keep up a slow rate of fire until Zero minus 1 hr. 40 mins.

6. **LEWIS GUNS.** The Lewis Gun teams in the front line will co-operate with fire towards the flanks sweeping the enemy's front line, and endeavouring to keep down hostile machine gun fire. Precautions as to the personnel of raid will be carefully considered.

7. INFANTRY ACTION AND TIME TABLE.

    Zero minus 3 hours. Two men will be detailed to lay a white tape into No Man's Land to 30 or 40 yards from enemy front line.

    Zero minus 2 hours 5 minutes.
    Raiding party will be in position in our front line in fire bays to North of head of PALL MALL communication trench (This part of trench having been previously
        cleared of all troops not connected with raid.)

    Zero minus 2 hours.
    Party will get out of our trench, cross wire and lie down.

Appendix I. (Contd)

Zero - 1 hr. 55 mins.
Party will move forward to their objective (conformable to Barrage) via tape. Two pairs of scouts will be detached at tape end and move out to guard flanks 30 or 40 yards, halting, lying down, and remaining on 'qui vive' until raiders return. One man will be left at tape end to guide raiders return and bring in tape.

At Zero - 1 hr. 50 mins party will enter German trench.

At Zero - 1 hr 45 mins. party leaves enemy trench and returns.

8. SIGNALS. Watches will be synchronised with Brigade at 6 hours before Zero. The officer in charge will give signal to leave our trench, also the signal to advance at Zero - 1 hr 55 mins.
At Zero minus 1 hr 45 mins, 3 Green [red crossed out] Very Lights will be fired from our front line to recall party.

9. HEADQUARTERS & COMMUNICATIONS.
O.C. Raiding Party will be in communication with Battalion H.Q. from Left Company H.Q.

10. DRESS. Officers.   Knobkerry, revolver and 3 hand grenades.
    2 Sgts.   Hand wire cutters.
    8 bayonet   Rifles, bayonets, S.A.A. wire cutters,
    men.   3 hand grenades.
    8 bombers.   8 hand grenades, knobkerry.
    Tapeman.   3 hand grenades, knobkerry.
    3 electric torches will be carried among party.
    All will have faces and hands blacked.

11. COUNTERSIGN. A countersign will be issued.

12. PATROL RECONNAISSANCE. O.C. Raid will arrange for patrolling ground, examining enemy's wire, and issuing verbal instructions and information to T.M.O. and L.G.O.

                                (sd) A.D. REID, Major,
                        Commanding 7th R. Innis Fus.

Copy. No 1 49th Bde H.Q.
  "   2 O.C. Raid.
  "   3 File.

Appendix V

SECRET.   Copy No. 10.

16TH DIVISIONAL ARTILLERY.

OPERATION ORDER NO. 35.

Ref 1/10000 28.S.W.1
& 28.S.W.2. Edn 3 E.   8th January 1917.

1. 49th Infantry Brigade will carry out a Raid on 12th instant.

2. Object. to penetrate enemy's support line, capture machine guns, trench mortars and prisoners, and to ascertain state of trenches.

3. Area to be Raided. Enemy front line trench between N.24.c.85.55 and N.30.a.68.96 to a depth of approximately 250 yards - N.24.d.27.55 to N.30.B.28.97.

4. Preparation. Wire to be cut at various points along Brigade front by Trench Mortars. D/177 to assist in scattering wire cut by Trench Mortars.
    Gaps to be kept open by Stokes Mortars and Lewis Guns. 18-pdrs will fire occasional bursts on the gaps at night.
    Action of Trench Mortars will be covered by fire on O.P's by WYTSCHAETE Group.

5. Feint. From ZERO minus 10 minutes till ZERO, SPANBROEK Group will bombard enemy front trench and communication trenches between N.30.a.42.40 and N.30.a.12.04 with two 18-pdr Batteries, rate of fire, 2 rounds per gun per minute.

6. Artillery Support During Raid. There will be no Artillery Bombardment on main Raid front immediately preceding raid.
    The Raiding Party will be drawn up in front of our wire before ZERO, and at ZERO will move forward and enter the enemy trenches.
    At ZERO PLUS 5 MINUTES a box barrage will be formed round the area to be raided. The Heavy Artillery will co-operate to mask the fire of Machine Guns from trenches in rear.
    Artillery objective are shown in the attached table.
    Fire will be maintained until the raiding party return to our trenches.
    Probable duration of raid 30 minutes.

7. SPANBROEK Group. A small party will also enter trenches between N.30.a.42.40 and N.30.a.12.04 and will remain not longer than 5 minutes.
    The two SPANBROEK Group Batteries at ZERO will lift at 50 yards a minute to the following line N.30.c.05.87 to N.30.c.50.90 to N.30.a.70.15 and will continue at one round per gun per minute until ZERO plus 10 minutes.

ACKNOWLEDGE.

(sd) H.H. JOLL; Major, R.A.
Issued at 12.45 p.m.   Brigade Major, 16th Div. Arty.

Copies to:-

    1. Spanbroek Group.   11. 16th Div "G"
    2. Wytschaete Group.   12. 41st Div. Arty.
    3. Vierstraat Group.   13. 36th Div Arty.
    4. D.T.M.O. 16th Div.   14. R.A. IX Corps.
    5.)   15. No. 1 Sqdn R.F.C.
    6.) H.A. IX Corps.   16 No. 5 Kite Balloon Coy.
    7.)   17 War Diary.
    8) 47th Inf Bde.   18)
    9   48th Inf. Bde.   19) File.
    10   49th Inf. Bde   20

Appendix V (Contd)

SECRET.

SPANBROEK Group.	16th Div "G"
WYTSCHAETE Group.	41st Div. Arty.
VIERSTRAAT Group.	36th Div Arty.
D.T.MO.16th Div.	R.A. IXth Corps.
H.A. IXth Corps (3)	No. 1 Sqdn R.F.C.
47th Inf.Bde.	No. 5 Balloon Coy.
48th Inf.Bde.	War Diary.
49th Inf.Bde.	File.

16th D.A. NO.R.2573. 9-1-17.

Reference 16th Divisional Artillery Operation Order No. 35 dated 8th January, 1917, paras 5 and 7 :-

(1) The action of the SPANBROEK Group has now been advanced by two hours.

(2) The bombardment mentioned in para 5 will now commence at ZERO minus 2 hours and 10 minutes.

Para 7. At ZERO minus 2 hrs the two SPANBROEK Batteries will lift and continue their fire until ZERO minus 1 hr and 30 minutes.

(3) In table of Artillery Objectives for 6" Hows. substitute 60-pdr Guns.

One 9.2 in. How will engage the work at N.24.d.99.15.

(4) 16th Divisional Artillery Groups will acknowledge.

(sd) H.H.JOLL, Major, R.A.
Brigade Major, 16th Div Artillery.

Appendix V (Contd)

SECRET.

SPANBROEK Group.	16th Div "G"
WYTSCHAETE Group.	41st Div Arty.
VIERSTRAAT Group.	36th Div Arty.
D.T.M.O. 16th Div.	R.A. IX Corps.
H.A. IX Corps.	No. 1 Sqdn R.F.C.
47th Inf.Bde.	No. 5 Balloon Coy.
48th Inf.Bde.	War Diary.
49th Inf.Bde.	File.

16th D.A. No. R.2573/1.   9-1-17.

Reference 16th Divisional Artillery No. R.2573 dated 9-1-17. Paras 1 and 2 are now cancelled.

The action of the SPANBROEK GROUP will be as follows :-

(1) ZERO minus 2 hours to ZERO minus 1 hour 50 minutes Bombardment of front trench.

(2) At ZERO minus 1 hour 50 minutes lift at 50 yards a minute on to second objective.

(3) Rate of fire from ZERO minus 1 hour 50 minutes to ZERO minus 1 hour 45 minutes 9 rounds per Battery per minute.

From ZERO minus 1 hour 45 minutes to ZERO minus 1 hour 40 minutes 6 rounds per Battery per minute.

(4) At ZERO minus 1 hour 40 minutes fire will cease.

(5) Objectives remain unchanged.

(6) 16th Divisional Artillery Groups will acknowledge.

(sd) H.H. JOLL, Major, R.A.

Brigade Major, 16th Div. Artillery.

Appendix VI

A. STOKES GUNS.   SCHEME FOR TRENCH MORTAR BOMBARDMENTS

FEINT.

No. of Gun.	Time.	Rate.	First Target.	Total.
			(20 yds of trench at)	
S.A.3.	Zero - 2 hrs to Zero - 1 hr 50 mins.	15 rds per gun per min.	N.30.a.12.04.	150
S.B.2.			N.30.a.30.15.	"
S.B.3.			N.30.a.33.20.	"
S.C.1.			N.30.a.33.39.	"
S.C.2.			N.30.a.43.40.	"
S.C.3.	do	5 rds per gun per min	N.30.a.50.35.	50
S.D.1			N.30.a.35.55.	"
S.D.2			N.30.a.75.50.	"
			Second Target.	
S.A.3.	Zero - 1 hr. 50 mins to Zero - 1 hr 35 mins.	5 rds per gun per min.	N.30.c.50.37.	75
S.B.2.			N.30.c.32.92.	"
S.B.3.			N.30.a.37.05.	"
S.C.1.			N.30.a.37.20.	"
S.C.2.			N.30.a.70.23.	"
S.C.3.	do	15 rds per gun per min.	N.30.a.50.65.	225
S.D.1.			N.30.a.65.55.	"
S.D.2.			N.30.a.75.50.	"

Total...1800.

RAID.

No. of Gun.	Time.	Rate.	Target.	Total.
S.C.3.	Zero plus 5 min. to Zero plus 35 mins.	5 rds per gun per min.	N.30.a.75.77.	150.
S.D.1.			N.30.a.50.80.	150.
S.D.2.			N.30.a.30.80.	150.

Total 450.

Grand Total.....2250 rds.

(sd) H.L.Hornby, Capt,
O.C. 29th T.M. Group.

Appendix VI)Contd)

B. 2" TRENCH MORTARS. SCHEME FOR TRENCH MORTAR BOMBARDMENT.

EINT.

No.of Gun.	Time.	Rate.	First Target.	Total.
T.B.4	Zero -2 hrs to Zero -1 hr 50 mins.	1 rd per gun per minute.	N.30.a.12.04 to N.30.a.30.33	10
T.C.2.	Zero -1 hr 50 mins.	do	N.30.a.30.33 to N.30.a.42.40 Buildings at PECKHAM.	10
T.C.3.	do	do		10
T.C.4.	do	do		10
			Second Target.	
T.B.4.	Zero -1 hr 50 mins to Zero -1 hr 35 mins.	1 rd per gun per minute.	N.30.c.50.87 to N.30.a.67.02	15.
T.C.2.	do	do	N.30.a.67.02 to N.30.a.70.23 Buildings at PECKHAM.	15.
T.C.3.	do	do		15
T.C.4.	do	do		15
			Total	100.

RAID.

No.of Gun.	Time.	Rate.	Target.	Total.
T.C.3.	Zero plus 5 to Zero plus 35	1 rd per 2 min per gun.	Buildings at PECKHAM.	15
T.C.4.				15.
			Total	30.

Grand Total...130.

(sd) H.L. Hornby, Captain,
O.C. 49th T.M. Group.

Appendix XII

49TH MACHINE GUN COMPANY.   ORDERS FOR RAID.

	FEINT.			RAID.	
Gun.	Time.	From.	To.	Time.	
1	Zero - 2 hrs to Zero - 1 hr.40 mins.	O.19.b.40.05.	O.19.b.05.70.	Zero - 5.	As in Feint Raid.
2.	do	Barrage SPANBROEKMOLEN behind Reserve Line.		do	N.30.b.05.75. N.30.a.75.20.
3.	do	Barrage HAKDELSTEDE Reserve Line.		do	O.19.c.9.4 O.19.c.9.9.
4.	do	N.24.d.95.50	O.19.d.40.95.	do	As in Feint Raid.
5.	do	PICK HOUSE		do	do
6.	do	N.30.d.55.35.	O.19.c.97.40.	do	do
7.	do	N.30.d.05.95	N.30.c.92.10.	do	do
8.	do	SCOTT FARM.	O.25.a.45.60 O.25.a.90.20.	do	do

Long bursts - 4 belts per gun.   All long bursts till Raid ended.

(sd) R. Le Butt, Major,
O.C. 49th Machine Gun Company.

Appendix VIII.

SIGNAL COMMUNICATIONS.

(1) For preliminary raid : line from Brigade to Battalion will be reserved for use of 49th Infantry Brigade Staff: line from Battalion H.Q. to Company H.Q. for use of O.C. Battalion to O.C. Raid.

(2) For main Raid; there will be a direct line from 49th Infantry Brigade Staff to O.C. Raid in VIA GELLIA. O.C. Battalion will be connected to both Raid Commanders by duplicated lines. Raid Commanders will be connected to raiding parties by wire. Drums revolving noiselessly on wooden frames will be fixed in parapet, and wires so arranged that signallers can communicate by means of a simple code while crossing to enemy line. In case wires are cut, an attempt will be made to get through visually by means of a special signalling lamp.

9-1-17.

(sd) H.E.L.PORTER, 2/Lieut,
O.C. Brigade Signals.

Appendix IX

TIME TABLE.

Zero Time

Time.

Zero - 2 hours to Zero - 1 hr. 50 mins.	Bombardment of enemy's front line N.30.a.42.40 to N.30.a.12.04.
Zero - 1 hr. 50 mins.	Barrage will creep back to Support Line and there remain. Small party enter enemy trenches.
Zero - 1 hr. 45 mins.	Party return. Barrage to continue another 5 minutes - i.e. until Zero - 1 hr. 40 mins.
Zero - 5 minutes.	Raiding Parties form up outside our wire.
Zero.	Raiding Parties move forward.
Zero + 5 minutes to Zero + 35 minutes.	Raiding Parties enter enemy lines and box barrage is opened round the area to be raided.
Zero + 35 minutes.	Recall Signal.

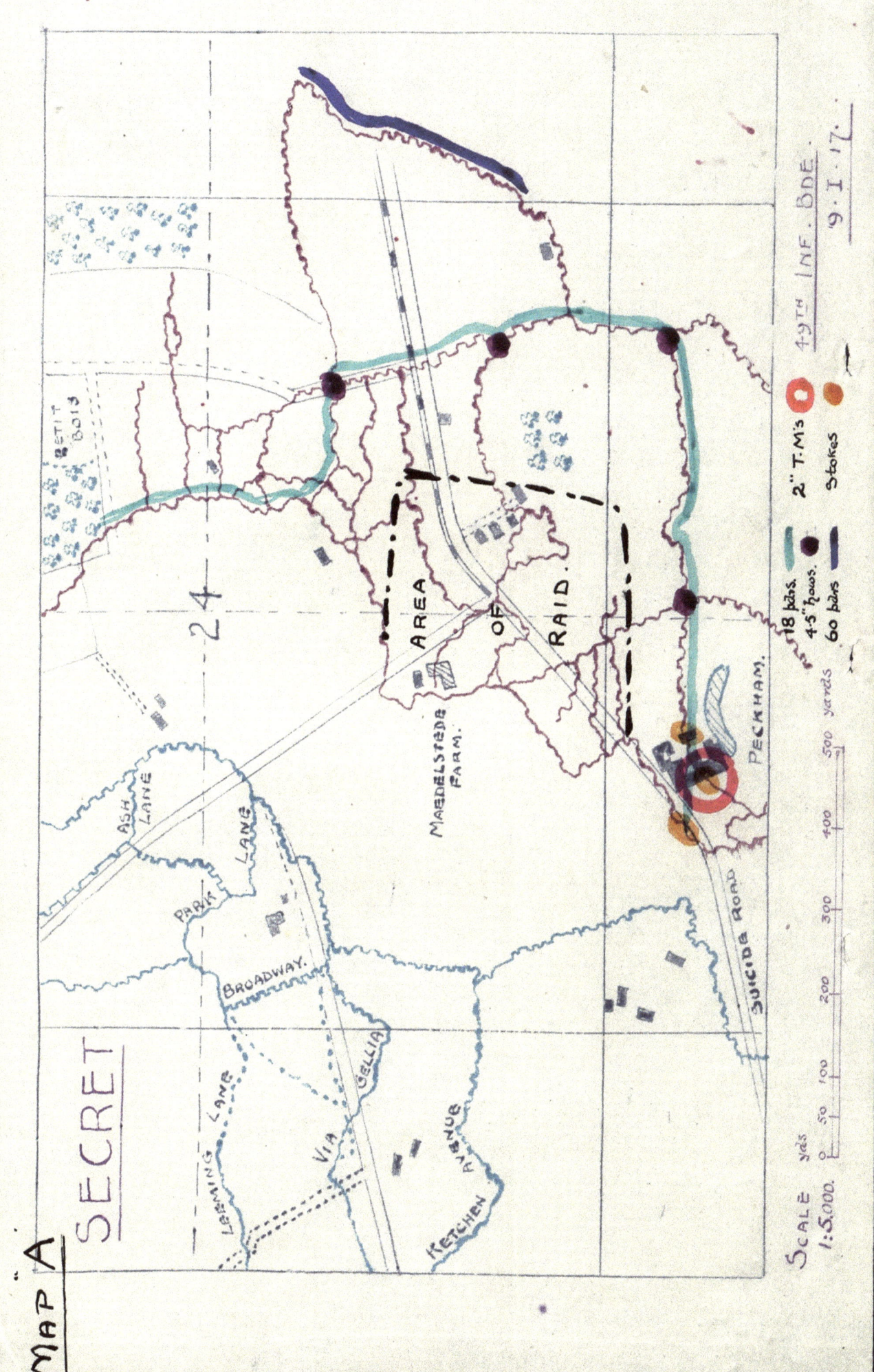

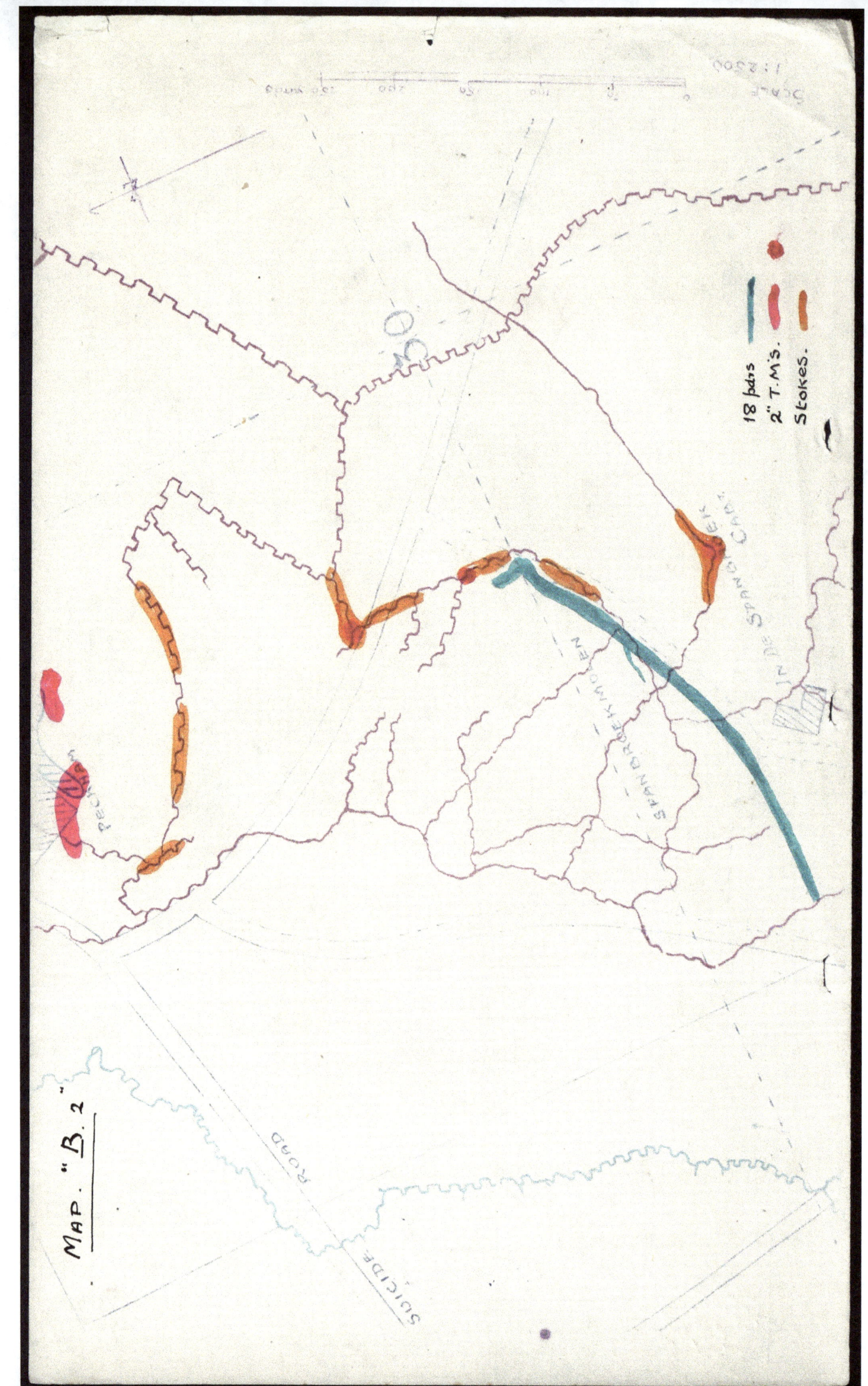

www.ingramcontent.com/pod-product-compliance
Lightning Source LLC
Chambersburg PA
CBHW081354160426
43192CB00013B/2407